# Under
## the
# Influence

MARGARET BLANCHARD

ISBN 978-1-0980-7259-9 (paperback)
ISBN 978-1-0980-7260-5 (digital)

Christian Faith Publishing, Inc.
832 Park Avenue
Meadville, PA 16335
www.christianfaithpublishing.com

Printed in the United States of America

*Under the Influence* is dedicated to my husband, Lt. Col. Larry Blanchard Esquire, with gratitude and unparalleled appreciation for his love and support in all my endeavors, for using his expertise as an avid reader, as well as his aptness as he reads the manuscript and questions what readers might not understand and make appropriate modifications. Thank you, husband, for being my consummate teammate. Much of this is possible because of you.

To my niece and prayer partner, Evelyn Loretta Taylor, your excitement was encouraging, as was your insatiable appetite to hear more, as you traveled with me throughout this journey. You kept me on track. You listened to me daily, following our morning devotions and helped me to better write from a reader's perspective. You were always there to assure me when some vital points needed to be simplified. Thank you for never holding back.

I thank God for the Holy Spirit's constant reminders of Proverbs 3:5–6: *"Trust in the Lord with all your heart: do not depend on your own understanding. Seek His will in all you do, and He will show you which path to take."* Thank you, Holy Spirit, for overriding my flawed understanding, pouring into me, and directing my path as I traveled into some desolate spaces. Thank you for enabling me to write this manuscript and expediting my understanding of being the branch and the Lord is the vine, and apart from Him, I can do nothing.

To My Pastor: Reverend, Doctor Sabin P. Strickland of Pleasant Hill Baptist Church, Roswell, Georgia; for anointed teachings and unabridged spiritual guidance. Under your leadership, I have feasted on fresh manner from heaven for over two decades. During that time, I have grown in leaps and bounds. This book was possible because you encouraged me to plunge deeper into Spiritual things. The debt of gratitude that I owe to you can never be paid in full in this life.

# Preface

Independence is an inherited trait of all mortal beings. The desire to influence the course of other people's lives is built into their DNA. But human beings were not created to be independent. They were created to be interdependent. Within the innermost sanctum of every mortal being lives a *natural* inclination for companionship. That's because mortal beings were created to depend on a reliable entity for support. Interdependence represents a safe bond that exists between two or more people. Within the confines of those bonds, each can rely on the other without either party losing his autonomy. But from the cradle to the grave people *fight* to be free from outside influence. The engagement involved in seeking independence can cause people to fall prey to the enemy of God and mankind, especially if they depend on unreliable entities for companionship.

*Under the Influence* is about the ongoing war between good and evil. All mortal beings live, move, and have their beings in worlds inhabited by physical and spiritual beings. Within those worlds are kings and kingdoms, controlled by leaders whose purposes are contradictory in nature. Inhabitants within the *earthly* world consistently witness scenes from that perpetual war within the spiritual world being played out on the screen within the earth. Unfortunately, very few of them realize that they are participants in that war whether they want to be or not. It's not something that people sign up for. Everyone was born into it.

The fierce fight between good and evil is demonstrated in the world by people's attitudes, actions, and love (or lack thereof) for each other. Graciousness is pitted against maliciousness in an unrestrained manner, especially among politicians during an election year! Proposed *leaders* cynically compete for the *power to control* citizens rather than honorably represent their wishes. *Under the Influence* is also about power, influence, and the responses of average people to propaganda versus truth, brainwashing versus authentic knowledge, and the overall impact that their choices can have on their lives. Those who are aware of the rationales behind the ongoing spiritual war will probably understand the motivation of the entities involved.

The purpose of *Under the Influence* is to further enlighten them. It is the hope that those who *might not be* acquainted with the didactics of this warfare will become enlightened after reading this arrangement.

*Under the Influence* consist of a variety of scenarios about spiritual beings existing within the *natural* and spiritual worlds. Regrettably, many scholarly people have little or no knowledge about the archenemy of God and his power to influence them. It was through an account of a *believer,* whose mind had been invaded by an evil spirit, that the author was inspired to write *Under the Influence.* The evil spirit had cunningly altered the believer's behavior without him ever knowing that such thing was even possible. He was aware of a few *strange* and *different* things occurring in his life. His attitude had subtly changed, and he seemed to have lost his ability to make principled choices. Wanting to help him, I went to the most powerful source available to me—the Word of God. I was divinely directed to a well-known Bible verse: "*Trust the Lord with all of your heart; do not depend on your own understanding. Seek His will in all you do and He will show you the path to take*" (see Proverbs 3:5). The author's trust and His guidance will be revealed throughout this script.

In each episode, a brief import of the topics to be discussed will be given. *Figurative* storylines about *imaginary* people, places, and incidents will be woven into each chapter. There will also be *much* authentic, positive, biblical data woven into each storyline. Biblical interjections will be disbursed throughout the script, which serve as solutions, aimed at deactivating the venom spewed out by evil spirits. Biblical inferences and quotations will be taken from the Living Bible (unless otherwise indicated).

This document will lead readers through some unchartered pathways regarding subjects about religion, politics, and education. Other life-changing information, which affects the lives of people from all walks of life, will be included as well. Some of the most outstanding reasons for the adversary's desire for the power to control will be discussed extensively throughout *Under the Influence*. The author will speak much about the omnipotent spiritual entity who has absolute control over the earth and everything in it, including devil, the overseer of evil spirits.

Almost every spiritually adverse issue discussed herein will be followed by a spiritually inspired resolution. There will be revelations of some malicious tactics used by the devil to influence the minds of behaviors of others, within whom he can find the slightest opening.

All the scenarios are fictitious as well as the names and places depicted herein. But the biblical disclosures and quotations are true. Optimistically, the developments within the covers of this document will reveal at least a bird's-eye view of what it really means to be *Under the Influence*.

# Spiritual Realms, Rulers, and You

Spiritual realms and rulers are not conversational terms that people are accustomed to. Therefore, a bit of clarification of the terms will be reviewed. Realm is spoken of more often as a territory, domain, sphere, or kingdom. They all refer to certain places of activities overseen by a ruler. It has been written that each domain is occupied by good and evil spirits simultaneously. Spiritual realms are ruled by a reigning spiritual ruler that controls the activities within the realm that he reigns over.

In this present age, there are two *governing* entities that most people are familiar with: the overall supreme spirit of the true and living God, who rules over the universe and everything and everyone in it; and the subordinate ruling spirit, who is the devil. The devil's domain is the natural earthly realm, but he is not confined to that realm. The perpetual spiritual warfare referenced here and there is all about who will influence mortal man's mind.

The journey through spiritual territories, and how all this affects you, might trigger many questions. To get a simple grasp of heavenly and earthly spaces, mentally travel outside the city limits for a moment.

You are encouraged to leave the city limits because within the city limits, the artificial lights are so bright until they overshadow the magnificent display of lights in the sky. Clear everything insignificant from your mind and focus the massive number of lights flickering across the sky. Every now and then, you might notice a heavenly body streaking across the sky millions of miles away. Those heavenly bodies have been dubbed falling stars.

There is an entire cosmos that exists outside Earth. The heavens, the sky, the spaces in between, and the atmosphere that mortals are most familiar with is known as the universe. The universe has been described by scientist and researchers as a collection of all things that exist in space, including a countless number of stars, planets, clouds, and gases separated by empty spaces in rotation. The rotary motion is determined by the one who created them all. Although human beings could never count all the stars in the sky, the psalmist wrote, *"He* (God) *counts the stars and call them all by name"* (see Psalm 147:4). Mankind has made numerous attempts to explore other planets and have collected much data from their surveys. When I asked, *"What are they looking for?"* the Lord clearly stated that *"The Lord our God has secrets known to no one. We are not accountable for them"* (see Deuteronomy 29:29). Whether other planets are among those secrets, I cannot say. Based on that proclamation, information within this script will be confined to things within the realms and rulers of the physical and spiritual world within the earth and in the heavens. All spirits live, move, and have their beings within an unseen world. They have the ability to influence the thoughts, principles, and behaviors of inhabitants within the physical world.

There seems to be more than one realm within heaven. God, in his infinite wisdom, chose to reveal himself in one of those realms to a dedicated saint worthy of such profound blessings. The Apostle Paul gives an account of such occasion: *"I will reluctantly tell about visions and revelations from the Lord! I was caught up into the third heaven some years ago. Whether I was in the body or out of the body, I don't know; only God knows. But I do know that I was caught up in paradise and heard things so astounding that they cannot be expressed in words, things no human is allowed to say"* (see 2 Corinthians 21–4). Some theologians have described three heavenly realms. Their information strongly suggests that the throne of God is in the third heaven. Believers don't have to be significantly concerned with that because their relationship with God is based on trust. They need to know that God is not a *physical* being. He is omnipotent (almighty, all-powerful, and invincible), omnipresent (universal, ever-present, and all-encompassing), and omniscient (all-knowing). While his throne might be in heaven, his presence is everywhere.

Within the spiritual world, the adversary (who himself is an evil spirit), along with the angels who rebelled against God, has their own kingdom. *The devil is the commander* (ruler) *of powers in that unseen world. He is the spirit at work in all the hearts of those who refuse to obey God* (see Ephesians 2:2). The saints of God *know* that the world in which they live is under the domination of the evil one (see 1 John 5:19). But they *should* understand that God is in control of the devil.

The devil's power is limited, and his time as commander-in-chief of the physical world is temporary. The revelator wrote: *"Then the devil, who deceived the people, was thrown down into the fiery lake of burning sulfur, joining the beast and the false prophet. There they will be tormented day and night forever and ever"* (see Revelations 20:10). Jude also reminds the saints that *"the angels who did not stay within the limits of authority God gave them, but left the place where they belonged, are kept securely chained in darkness. They are waiting for that great Day of Judgment"* (see Jude 6). There is some value in knowing something about the devil, which will be revealed.

It might be challenging for mortal beings to grasp the concept of God's involvement in the functions within the physical world and things occurring within the heavenly realms simultaneously, especially unbelievers. Some mortals believe that just because they can't see things with their natural eyes and touch them with their human hands, they don't exist. That's why it is of the utmost importance for believers and nonbelievers alike to acquire a working knowledge of who God is. It is written that *"For ever since the world was created people have seen the earth and sky. Through everything God made, people can see His invisible qualities, eternal power and divine nature"* (see Romans 1:20). Mortals can feel the wind blowing and see flowers blooming, yet they cannot see the wind, but they see the proof of the invisible God in the blooming flowers. Humans see flashes of lightning and hear the roars of thunder, which further provides proof of God's power and control over nature. *"The rain and snow come down from heaven and stay on the ground to water the earth, which causes grain to grow. Although mortals cannot see what occurs when the rain and snow saturates the ground and germinate seeds, they see the miraculous results"* (see Romans 55:10). Buds from the seeds sprout up from the ground and provide growth for food. Do you know how that happens in the darkness under the ground? You do know that something happens though!

As you venture on through this journey of the earth's domain, it is of critically significance that you *never underestimated* the power of the devil. Although mortal beings encounter evil spirits as well as good spirits, the essence of their own spirit is their minds. Everyone *can be* influenced by either spirit, depending on a multitude of variables, the most important one being their salvation status. Take this into consideration: Every human being was born a sinner from the moment their mothers conceived them. Therefore, the human mind and body are solely accustomed to sin, which is the nature they inherited from the devil.

The devil and his demons work hard to keep carnal-minded humans from shedding that old nature through redemption. He wants them to remain under his influence. He also works diligently on the minds of believers to persuade them to follow him, and he has enough power to do that too! The devil and all the rebellious angels (demons) who were thrown down from heaven with him know that they will spend eternity in hell. Their game plan is to convince their victims (whose minds they have manipulated) to rebel against God. But God really wants everyone to be saved from an eternity in hell and to understand the truth. That was his reason for putting on the heavy garment of flesh and dying that horrendous death on the cross!

Even after people have accept the Lord's invitation for salvation, they are not exempt from the *ability* to sin. The devil appeals to the mind and body, over which he gained control of when he convinced the first couple to sin. That is why saints of God are cautioned to surrender their bodily urges and mental hindrances to the Lord as often as necessary (see Romans 12:1). Once a person surrenders his all to the Lord, his mind can become renewed by a divine transformation process.

God loves his created beings and wants them to love him back because they want to. He gave mortal beings the precious gift of making independent decisions (free will). The devil knows all about that will. Once he has invaded their mind, he begins to work on their God-ordained will. The devil doesn't just want to use people. He wants to possess, dominate, and control them.

Further on into this journey through *Under the Influence,* numerous means and methods, used by the devil to gain and maintain supreme authority over mortals, will come to fruition. But first, allow me to present an abridged summary of the ruler (ruler) of the unseen worlds.

God reveals himself to those who have accepted Jesus as a Savior and yielded to his lordship. But until mortal beings accept the invitation to open the door of their hearts and invite him in, they *cannot* know him. *"People who aren't spiritual can't receive the truths from God's Spirit"* because those truths are spiritually revealed (see 1 Corinthians 2:14). Actually, *knowing God* comes through revelation knowledge from the accounts of him in the Bible. We know from the book of Genesis that *"God is Creator of heaven and earth; the waters and all that are in them. The earth is the Lords and everything in it. The world and all the people in it belong to Him"* (see Psalm 21:1). God is the one and only Supreme Being. He declared of himself: *"Heaven is my throne and the earth is my footstool"* (see Isaiah 66:1). God is the major focal point and incentive of believers' faith.

Occasionally, believers reference the Godhead, the triune God, and the Trinity when speaking of the deity. Simply put, deity means divine nature, or in essence, the nature of God. Godhead speaks of the sovereign, integral, and undivided existence of the Father, the Son and Holy Spirit as one. Tri, preceding any word, means three; but in the divine assertion, when meshed with *une,* the word triune is an indication of the unity of three beings with the same God-orientated purpose. Therefore, as we see, these terms used are interchangeable, perhaps their undertakings might seem distinctive, but their determinations, principles, and intentions are communal and mutually shared. Everything originates from the one God. Example. God the Father created all things that exist. God the Son donned a fleshly body to bring about salvation. The Holy Spirit is representative of the Spirit of Jesus as an indwelling source of power within human beings following Jesus's death. They all exist because of the great love they have for humankind. The motive for everything that the Godhead did (and does) is to guide humankind through becoming *positioned* to spend eternal life with the Lord.

God's characteristic traits are many. Among them are he is infinite or self-existence, without a beginning or end. God *"existed before anything else and holds all creation together"* (see Colossians 1:17). He is absolutely whole and unimpaired within himself. Therefore, he does not *need* anything. *"The Father has life within himself and He has granted the same life-giving power to His Son"* (see John 5:17). The Lord is always the same, which makes him unchangeable, undisputable, irreversible, and perpetual. *"I the Lord do not change"* (see Malachi 3:6). He is the total embodiment of a love so deep that mortal beings cannot totally understand it. However, the mission of getting to know him must be experienced on a personal level. He delights in revealing himself through his Word. Once you begin that journey, you will want to know more and more about him. Believers can truly focus on this promise: *"The Holy Spirit, whom the Father will send in Jesus name, will teach you all things"* (see John 14:26). To truly know God, one has to interact with him on an intimate spiritual level. This type of relationship can only be developed through commitment, trust, and actually working at fulfilling your purpose in accordance with his will for your life. You must begin by doing what he did, deny yourself, take up your cross, and follow him.

Many times, adjustments must be made to your present lifestyle as you learn how to walk with the Lord. On the journey through life with him, you will become so familiar with him until you will know his voice in a spiritual way. You will sense his presence with you, and you will learn to believe as Jesus believed. He will become your most trusted friend. *"You must have the same attitude that Christ Jesus has"* (see Philippians 2:5) to reach that level of growth.

All the knowledge shared about God will seem foolish and insignificant to unbelievers. Anyone who hasn't accepted Jesus as their Savior and *positioned* themselves for him to become the Lord over their lives are considered unbelievers. Even now, the Lord is saying to you: "Look! *I stand at the door* (of your heart) *and knock.*

*If you hear my voice and open the door I will come in and we can share a meal together as friends"* (see Revelations 3:20). Jesus is addressing all unbelievers, including churchgoers who have been misled by false prophets, gullible people who have forms of godliness but denies the power of God, defrauded congregants with itchy ears, as well as misinformed congregants who fail to study to prove themselves to God. Everyone in those categories is in a position to fall prey to the manipulative tactics of the devil.

Some of the most significant weapons the devil uses against mortals include unbelief, denial, self-aggrandizing attitudes, and love of the world and the things in it. There is an inordinate number of people, believers and unbelievers alike, who don't believe that the devil has the power to infiltrate their minds. There might be an equal number of people who deny information regarding demon possession. Self-aggrandizing people are more like the devil than they realize.

Perhaps a quick review of who you're dealing with in the devil might inspire you to open that door to your heart for Jesus to come in. Satan is a spiritual being whose position, power, and province are under the adjudication of God. He is in no way considered parallel to God. But he is powerful enough to wield a significant amount of influence over human behavior and human events. He has many names that correspond to his characteristic traits. Some of the more common names include the devil, which is an evil spirit that defames, vilifies, and slanders the characters of mortal beings. Lucifer, which means light bearer, but he is said to have been the one behind the philosophical declaration encouraging other angelic beings to challenge God. Satan's name means adversary, antagonist along with other traits that he exhibits. They all work together against God's purpose and plans for his people.

Satan and all the angels who followed his leadership in challenging God were ejected from heaven. Jesus told his disciples: *"I saw Satan fall from heaven like lightening"* (see Luke 10:18). He has an Army of demonic spirits working on his behalf to do the following to humans, particularly believers. *Kill* their confidence, support, and loyalty; *steal* the crown that the Lord has laid up in heaven for believers. He knows that *"God blesses those who patiently endure testing and temptation. Afterward they will receive the crown of life that God has promised to those that love Him"* (see James 1:12). He wants to *destroy* the character of believers and, ultimately, determine their destiny. All this is to prevent them from doing God's will.

Before the fall of man, his soul was pure and free of corruption because it was divinely breathed into him by God. When God created the man's body from the dust, it was just a body until *"God breathed the breath of life into him and he became a living soul"* (see Genesis 2:7). God gave the man dominance over the earth and all the living creatures therein. However, once the serpent, influenced by the devil, deceived the first couple, the seed of the man became corrupt. The purity of his soul was tarnished, which spiritually separated him from God. That's how the devil gained control over the physical world *for a season.*

Well, when Jesus came in the flesh, died on the cross, and ascended back to his Father with *all power* in his hands, the devil's power over the human's nature was in jeopardy. The acts of Christ brought forth the plan of salvation. The essence of man could be connected to God the Father, again through Jesus Christ! The devil is fervently fighting to recapture the soul of man.

The soul of man is that sensitive, emotional, discerning, and affectionate part of his inner being. The seat of the senses, desires, and appetites are said to reside there. Every living human being has a soul. The soul differs from the spirit. In that the spirit, part of man connects him to God through Jesus Christ. This comes to fruition by human by choice.

Consequences for all the participants in the fall of man were issued. To the serpent, the Lord said, *"Because you have done this you will crawl on your belly as long as you live. And I will cause hostility between you and the woman and between your offspring and her offspring. He will strike your head and you will strike his heel"* (see Genesis 3:15). This promise was fulfilled in Christ's victory over Satan. All believers share in that victory. Satan and his demons have already been defeated. And they know it too. Human beings have the choice to be defeated with him, or share in the victory that Christ has made available to them.

The creator, who is supreme ruler of all things, divinely established a mandate to bring about orderliness within all the provinces and other dimensions. When God reinhabited the earth following the flood, he also set things in order: "*As long as the earth endures, seedtime and harvest, cold and heat, summer and winter, day and night will never cease*" (see Genesis 8:22 NJV). The times and seasons, created by him in the beginning, were reestablished.

Nothing occurs arbitrarily or accidentally within the universe without God's knowledge. God has prearranged everything and everyone to fulfill specific purposes. Everyone has a distinct space, which is a divinely arranged place and a resolute purpose for being brought forth. Not many people are well-acquainted with their distinctive *selves* because they've allowed other people and circumstances to define them. When people fit themselves into *humanly dictated* molds, it prevents them from becoming the people they were created to be.

The unique distinctive *space* allocated to each individual represents *that* individual's particular scope of significance in God's panoramic plan for his people. Mortal beings were born to achieve purpose(s) within the space earmarked just for them. An individual's precise space can be compared to lanes on a freeway. No matter how many lanes any given freeway has, visible lines define the space each vehicle should occupy. The law of physics says that no two objects can occupy the same space at the same time. Yet some vehicles move into occupied lanes more often than we'd like to mention. Generally, this results in a collision because the law *cannot* be *defied* without adverse consequences. Sometimes the occupant driving in his lane *chooses* to move over and give up his lane, but in so doing, it is very possible that he might veer off his charted course into another car.

The idea is to stay in your divinely appointed lane (space) that was designed just for you. If you choose to move over for another "*driver,*" *you are relinquishing your* God-allocated *power.* You will need divine supernatural power to fulfill your resolute prearranged *purpose* in the time and place apportioned to you. The Lord has "*charted the path ahead of you and He will tell you where to stop and rest. Every moment He knows where you are*" (see Psalm 139:3–4 TLB). So as long as you stay in your lane, you shouldn't be anxious about others moving around you within the world. This is done *by faith* because you have God's power, protection, and provisions when your will aligns with his will. God brought you forth in the fullness of *his* time, placed you in the family of *his* choice for you to serve him at a precise time and place to fulfill a distinctive purpose.

Before God called Jeremiah to be a prophet, he knew beforehand that someone would be needed to foretell of the upcoming calamities of the nations. He brought forth Jeremiah, the son of a Hebrew priest and an unnamed godly mother, about seventeen years in advance. Jeremiah was like many of today's saints, hesitant and resistant, because he looked at his circumstances, instead of focusing on the Lord. But the Lord told Jeremiah, "*I knew you before you were formed in your mother's womb. Before you were born I set you apart to and appointed you as my prophet to the nations*" (See Jeremiah 1:5). Whenever God calls anyone to fulfill a purpose, he also equips them with everything they need to complete the divinely ordained task. Even if Jeremiah did not know that he was ready, God knew what he had invested in him.

A songwriter once wrote a song that said that no one has to stay in the shape that he's in. So it doesn't matter what shape you see yourself in. In God's eyesight, you are special. *Human beings were so special to God until He made them a little lower than the angels and crowned them with glory and honor. He gave them authority over all things* (see Hebrews 2:7). The Lord made all your delicate *inner* parts while knitting you together in your mother's womb. He watched you as you were being formed in utter seclusion. He saw you as *you* before you were born (see Psalm 139:13–16). Perhaps those things that cannot be seen with natural eyes, or touched with physical hands were being put in place to *determine your personal identity.* Those things might have included your personality, your divine gifts and talents, and everything else appointed for you to do according to God's plan for your life. You were created to love God just because you wanted to love God. Although human beings can never love God the way he loves them, he provided ways that they could show their love for him. "*If you love me obey my commandments. All who love me will do what I say"* (see John 14:15 and 23). He has affirmed that believers are the righteousness of God, not because of you but because of the Holy Spirit that lives in the inner most part of your being. God's righteousness opens up a myriad of supernatural doors for believers, such as revelation knowledge; permission to ask anything (within his will) in his name, and he will ask the Father to grant you the petition that you desire; and forgiveness of sins if you confess them. He will even heal a broken heart if a believer gives him all the pieces.

*"No eye has seen, no ear has heard, and no mind imagined what God has prepared for those who love Him"* (see 1 Corinthians 2:9). Nothing is ever hidden from him. He even knows your thoughts and still loves you! You were destined for heaven. *"Even before He made the world, God loved us and chose us in Christ, to be holy and without fault in His eyes"* (see Ephesians 1:4). Will you be able to see yourself like that?

Far too many people see themselves through human eyes and not always their own. We already discussed the law of physics. Still, there are believers and nonbelievers alike who cannot leave the past behind and live in the moment long enough to walk into their destiny. The past can be like a heavy ball attached to a thicker heavy chain and placed around one's ankle. That person is bound by the ball and chain of their past because it's too heavy to drag into the future that God has planned for them. Subsequently, they remain in bondage to their poor-me circumstances. Their divinely, purposely arranged destiny, which is determined by whether they accept or reject the totality of Jesus Christ, might never be realized. Everyone has an opportunity to accept Jesus as Savior and Lord. While the hope of most individuals is eternal life with the Lord, the *only* way to achieve that goal is through Jesus Christ on his terms. Jesus told his disciples, *"I am the way the truth and the life. No one can come to the Father except through me"* (see John 14:6). That quote is still true today and forevermore.

Some people mistake destiny for fate. Fate is one of those unavoidably incidents that will occur at some future point in everyone's life. Humankind cannot control their fate, nor do they have a choice in when or how fate brings about changes in their lives. Death is the unescapably fate of all human beings. The time to think about where you will spend eternity is while you are still alive. The choice to accept or reject Jesus Christ expires when your physical life comes to a close. If you're reading this, and you haven't made that decision, you still have time.

Humans are told to examine themselves. This process requires no special primping or preparations. Begin wherever you are. Don't drag in *who you think you are, or who you hope to be and not who they say you are*. It's not your outward appearances that you are assessing. It's your behavior, things you do when no one is looking. Include your motives for your actions words and deeds. Take a moment to ask yourself: Who are you glorifying? Yourself or God. Think back on how many times you've referenced yourself in a general conversation (I, me, and mine versus we, us, and *our*). Pay strict attention to your own works without comparing them to someone else's. Have you taken responsibility for your own attitude and approaches along with any other depraved habits that you might secretly harbor?

The objective should be to spiritually establish yourself so that you will not become deceitful, conceited, or mislead. Understand fully that God cannot be mocked. You will *always* reap whatever you sow. "*Those who live to satisfy their own sinful nature will harvest decay and death from their sinful* nature. *But those who live to please the Spirit will reap everlasting life from the Spirit…if they don't give up*" (see Galatians 6:4–7).

Some people are blessed with intellectual knowledge, ideal professions, financial security, and respectful statuses in their communities. Such *blessings* can cause them to become pompous, proud, and haughty. Without recognizing that all good gifts come down from heaven, their standings in the world *can* deviously take precedence over their devotion to the Lord. Without realizing the shift, they begin to regard the *idols* of fame, fortune, and self-interests more reverently than paying homage to God. Egocentric attitudes motivate them to put more and more energy into maintaining their cushy lifestyles, which leaves little or no time for worshiping God. It has been said that Lucifer was a most beautiful and brilliant created being until he became captivated by his own beauty, brilliance, and position. The very things that he was enchanted by became his downfall. The devil can slip a Luciferin mindset into any mind that is not focused on the Lord.

When one's mind has been pervaded by the enemy, he can be compared to a naive lamb being led to the slaughter. He has been undetectably influenced by the enemy to satisfy his own carnal nature. Oftentimes, the enemy seems to be whispering in their ears, *"You worked hard, and you deserve this time for yourself. Go on, have some fun!"* Even though believers have been cautioned about loving the world and the things in it, they don't really believe that the Lord is talking to him. Their minds are under the influence of the enemy whose purpose is to lead him away from the Lord.

Once upon a time, there was a wonderful young lady called Mary. She was the seventh child in a family that believed the seventh child was born for good fortune. Mary was an obedient child and believed that she was walking with the Lord as she grew in statue and wisdom. She did everything that *she thought* was right based on what she knew to be true. But Mary was a bit proud and began to mentally point out the faults of everyone else. One day, she heard the voice of the Lord telling her, *"The high places, he will bring down."* Mary begin to look around her and focus on friends and family members whom *she believe*d were committing all manner of acts of rebellion against the Lord. Mary even prayed fervently for these persons by name. She kept hearing the same voices over and over again, saying the same thing. Certain that the Lord was not talking to her, she prayed even more fervently for her family and friends

One day, the Lord gave the enemy permission to test her faithfulness. She found herself physically attracted to a *forbidden* male. Seemingly, she believed that she could cavort with this man for a season and ask for forgiveness and get right back into the good graces of the Lord. But before she realized it, she found herself wallowing in the messy situation and not looking for a way out, but she kept on praying.

One day, Mary came to her senses *because she never stopped praying.* When she actually *heard* the message from the Lord again, she knew that he was speaking to her. She immediately fell on her knees, repented, and lamented before the Lord for forgiveness. She apologized to the forbidden male for her ungodly behavior, and she was released from the bondage that had captivated her for a season. Mary learned that no one was exempt from the wiles of the devil and judging should be left up to the Lord. *She was cleansed from all unrighteousness* and found favor with the Lord!

Many believers wander away from the Lord. But he has made provisions for their return. They might come to understand the expression: What does it profit a man to gain the whole world and lose his soul (to the adversary)? One of God's commandments is "*You must not have any other god but me*" (see Exodus 20:3). That commandment is further reiterated as the most important commandment in the New Testament. "*You must love the Lord your God with all your heart all your soul all your mind and all your strength*" (see Mark 12:30). There will always be choices, as well as consequences, based on the decisions one make.

God is a Spirit, and those who worship him must do so in spirit and truth. Worship is so much more than lifting up *holy* hands and praising him in church. The fundamental nature of worship requires familiarity with God. Once one has *experienced* him in an interpersonal way and cherishes him with jubilant gratification, devotion, reverence, and adulation, worship inevitably flows from the heart. Love is on display as the believer serves God by *doing what he says.*

Worshiping of idols is quite different from humble reverential worship of God. As with most things under the adversary's control, worshipping of idols is done under the cloak of darkness. The joy of the Lord has been replaced with annoyance and irritation, especially when confronted about objectionable behavioral changes.

When human beings look *into* themselves from the inside out, they will probably find some unsettled things. With the understanding that no good thing dwells in the flesh, they should come to know that God created every individual to become great in his eyes. Jesus assures believers that he came to the earth as a man that they might have life with him in eternity as well as a bountiful life on earth. Abundance is not about stuff and things, professional achievements, and lavishness. The abundance that the Lord is referring to is flourishing spiritual riches of joy within the mind, body, and soul, and most of all, love. The Lord does not object to any of the things that human beings achieve. He just wants them to keep them in perspective. Don't put things over people and anything at all above God.

When God looks at you, he sees you through the eyes of Jesus. He knows that Jesus understands what it is like to live in the flesh. He wants you to see yourself through the eyes of Jesus. God, through Jesus Christ, can make us right in his sight. "*So there is no condemnation for those who belong to Christ. The power of the life-giving Spirit has freed you from the power of sin that leads to death*" (see Roman 8:1–2). There will be rebuking and punishment for those who commit sins, only because God loves you.

By now, you know there is a perpetual war going on in the world. The devil is fighting tooth and nail to possess your soul. God has enough power to protect you, provide for you, and empower you to resist the devil. You just have to believe it.

# Believe It, Perceive It, Receive It

Belief is representative of an individual's attitude regarding truth, lies theories, ideas, and concepts. What a person believes or disbelieves, in this instance, primarily involves the existence or nonexistence of certain tangible entities, which are discussed throughout this narrative. Perception can be explained as a sensible conclusion based on one's personal evaluation and understanding of what is presented to him. To receive something is to take into one's possession, or accept whatever he believes as true. Before receiving the benefits of grace, one has to understand and accept the principles and proof accurately presented to him.

Belief is closely related to trust and faith. The writer of Hebrews describes faith thusly: *"Faith is the confidence that what we hope for will actually happen; it gives assurance about things we cannot see"* (see Hebrews 11:1). A person's belief is usually based on how much he knows about a particular subject as well as his desire to accept proven truths. Before one can believe God or anything else, he must *acknowledge* that God, or a particular thing, exists. This kind of faith is acceptance of truth, although there might not be any tangible proof. But before anyone can actually consider the existence of spiritual beings in an unseen world, authentic knowledge from the Creator of all things must be accepted as true. It is difficult, if not impossible, for the natural unconverted mind to accept revelations from the Word of God. The issue of unbelief must be dealt with first. *"The message of the cross* (Word of God) *is foolish to those who are headed for destruction! But we who are being saved know it is the very power of God"* (see 1 Corinthians 1:18).

Unbelief is like a revolving door of the mind where the devil and his demons can go in and out at will. Once evil spirits enter into unbelievers' minds, they establish devious, evil attitudes much like their own and even invite other evil spirits in as well.

Once upon a time, a talented young woman called Vanity moved to a fast-paced city called Whimsical. This suited Vanity quite well since she had always lived her life in the fast lane. Vanity was gorgeous with more than a little wit and charm. Her extra-large brown eyes caught the attention of many bystanders, and she had learned to flutter her eyelashes to make her eyes even more noticeable. Her skin texture could be compared to a rich creamy dark-chocolate candy bar. Vanity was in her midthirties and the mother of two teenage daughters. She had been covertly persuaded to believe that she had no real value except her body and her melodious voice. She had been told that her skin tone was a disadvantage. Vanity had been blessed with a voice that could figuratively compete with that of a song bird. Because her complexion was a bit darker than her other siblings, she had been designated as the caretaker of her single mother and other siblings. She dutifully did what was demanded of her without murmuring or complaining.

Vanity's mother was known for entertaining male associates in her home, from whom she procured monetary favors. That was where Vanity learned early on in life that she could use her body as a means of taking care of herself financially. Like her mother, Vanity became a mother very early. Having no skills and no definite means of financial support, Vanity had enticed an older man to marry while she was in her teens. Thus, her education was cut short. She wanted to move away from the life she knew and begin a new life for herself and her children, but her Jezebel spirit followed her.

A Jezebel spirit is one of the devil's seductive spirits that ranks high on his pyramid of evil spirits. Jezebel refers to a queen by that name in the olden days. Queen Jezebel was noted for using her feminine wiles to turn her husband, the king, away from righteousness. She was also noted for killing the prophets of God, of which Elijah was one. The Jezebel spirit is among the most evil, ghastly, and cunning spirits within the devil's arsenal.

Vanity's husband's employment caused him to travel a lot. Vanity didn't fit in well with the other corporate wives. She decided to settle in Whimsical, where she met some people who attended a popular church there. She quickly attached herself to members in the choir, where she was readily received because of her masterful voice. She also met a few other godly women, whom she greatly admired. There was one petite woman, Faith, who was about a decade older than Vanity that she wanted to emulate. At first, Vanity tried to dress like Faith, walk like Faith, and carry herself like Faith. Faith seemed to be everything that Vanity wasn't but wanted to be. But the suppressed darkness, embedded within her demeanor, just kept popping up.

Vanity made a point of being in Faith's presence as often as possible. Faith was friendly and easy to talk to, so they became quick friends. Once she felt comfortable enough with Faith, Vanity began asking questions about her life and the overt light that seemed to radiate from her. Faith simply told her new friend, "That must be my inner spiritual light shining through!"

As Faith began to share simple things about life with Vanity, their friendship grew, and Faith became a mentor to the younger woman. Vanity was eager to learn and as eager to share her life's story with Faith. So she shared her past about using her body to attract men with money to support her lifestyle. She told Faith about the cordial relationship she shared with her husband and the meager financial allowance he gave her. Faith listened intently and told Vanity that God loved her and had a much better plan for her life. Vanity was overjoyed when she learned that she didn't have to stay in the shape that she found herself in at that moment. Although her perception of numerous issues had been darkened, Vanity began to earnestly seek the light, which she didn't believe was available to her in times past.

During the course of their developing relationship, a rumor arose among some of the church women involving an ill-omened incident about one of the newer female parishioners, Damiona. Vanity had developed a close friendship with Damiona. The rumor that Damiona used some form of black magic to manipulate one of the male officers of the church spread like wildfire. Damiona's intention was to make her particular male suitor jealous because he would not forsake his family to marry her. Her male suitor had avoided the traps that Damiona had set to bring him under her influence. So she set her sights on someone else within the church.

One day, Faith and Vanity were discussing the issue, and a disagreement arose between the two. Vanity attempted to defend her friend by immediately stating that she didn't believe in witchcraft. She accused the other women of being jealous of Damiona's beauty. She was indeed attractive!

Faith knew that Vanity was spiritually weak. She also knew that the enemy wanted to create division between her and Vanity, so she quickly ended the discussion. Knowing that Vanity was in dire needed of spiritual guidance, Faith gently asked Vanity if she believed that the Bible was inspired by God. Vanity answered, "Of course, I do!" Faith assured Vanity that she had no knowledge of Damiona's involvement on the dark spirits, but witchcraft was real. She shared this scripture with Vanity: "*When you enter the land that the Lord your God is giving you, be very careful not to imitate the detestable customs of the nations living there... And do not let your people practice fortune-telling, or use sorcery or interpret omens or engage in witchcraft*" (see Deuteronomy 18:10). Vanity was shocked! But she did not readily accept the concept, saying instead, "It didn't say anything about black magic." Faith assured her that black magic is spoken of, biblically, in the same category as witchcraft and sorcery. Practitioners of such evils have been empowered by the devil to summons evil supernatural powers for self-aggrandizing purposes. All those evils are considered to be *works of the flesh*, which include any and all *supernatural deeds not* empowered by the Holy Spirit. Works of the flesh are connected to the things in the world and what those things offer: *Cravings for physical pleasure and everything the eyes see and pride in achievements and possessions* (see 1 John 2:15–16). Seemingly, Vanity was basing her disbelief on her lack of authentic knowledge regarding such issues. However, she had a desire to know the truth and asked Faith to tell her more.

Faith knew that it would take time for Vanity to digest the new information that she was imparting. So she set up a time for a self-styled Bible review with Vanity so that she could position herself to perceive truth and accept it from the Word of God.

Before delving into the spiritually dark world controlled by the devil, Faith made sure Vanity had intentionally invited Jesus into her heart. Knowing that it was to the devil's advantage to keep Vanity in darkness, Faith wanted to be sure that the provisions and power of God would protect her young friend from falling into the tempter's snare.

After Faith learned of Vanity's redemption, she began her teaching sessions. First, Faith explained each biblical reference about witchcraft, sorcery, soothsayers, and seducing spirits in the simplest way possible. Faith began by giving her young friend a working definition of witchcraft, which included the practice of black magic for evil purposes. Black is indicative of dark powers. Magic means being in possession of power with the ability to influence one's behavior as well as the course of some events in their lives. Everyone involved evil crafts uses mystifying power from a supernatural force to dominate the minds of their victims. The devil, manifested in human form, uses feminine charms, enticements, divination, and a myriad of other tactics to achieve their goal. Since the devil is a spirit, he doesn't have a body, but he can implant his spirit within a human body.

Charms include magnetisms, mesmerisms, charismas, and magical enhancements to attract the attention of victims. Enticement is a method of luring a person into a tantalizing, arousing situation. Divination is divergence away from the purity or holiness or anything that is divine. Divination is more in line with fortune-telling and premonitions. Some of the portions and other intensifying substances used in black magic might also be hallucinogenic and/or hypnotic in nature. The primary objective of the captor is to cunningly gain entry into the mind and spirit of his prey. Evil practices are in direct association with demonic spirits. In a nutshell, initiators, seeking to influence other people in such dark manners, intentionally conjure up demonic spirit to empower them to perform their dark deeds.

Faith told Vanity the story about King Saul, whom God had appointed as the first King in Israel. "*Saul said to his advisors: Find a woman who is a medium so I can go and ask her what to do.* His request was: *I have to talk to a man who has died. Will you call up his spirit for me?"* (see 1 Samuel 28: 7–8). Saul's idea of kingship differed from that of the Lord. King Saul disobeyed the commands of the Lord. His loyalty seemed to have been to himself, and what he perceived to be a better plan. God perceived King Saul's acts of disobedience as rebellion, thus, comparing his rebellion to witchcraft. *"Rebellion is as sinful as witchcraft, and stubbornness as bad as worshiping idols"* (see 1 Samuel 15:23). Because of King Saul's involvement with the devil, God rejected him as king.

Vanity was mesmerized by what she had just read along with Faith. She asked, *"How do you know this stuff."* Faith told her that she had been studying the Bible for a long time but mostly because she was nosey and needed to see things for herself after hearing preachers preach about things that she had no knowledge about.

Faith told Vanity more about seducing spirits, saying, "Some women who choose to employ seducing spirits are compared to Jezebel in the Bible."

Vanity looked puzzled and asked, "What in the world is a seducing spirit?"

Faith told her that a seducing spirit represents an exclusive means of entrapping someone within Satan's kingdom. Jezebel used the power seduction to lure her husband away from appropriate behavior.

Having used her body to seduce male companions in the past, Vanity asked, *"So you mean to tell me that God sees me as having a Jezebel spirit?"*

"If you intentionally enticed someone from the path of uprightness and moral integrity and lured them away from morality and led them into to iniquity, the answer would be yes! The Lord sees that demonic behavior as sinful activity!"

Vanity appeared to be crushed because she had not yet learned the power of forgiving and being forgiven.

Faith shared with Vanity that she should not allow her past to shape her future. Faith simplified some Bible verses for Vanity saying, "When you are in Christ, and Christ is in you, and you stand before the judgment, Christ's presence will stand with you. As a believer, you have received righteousness from God by faith. So, in Christ, our sins have been forgiven and there in no condemnation" (see Romans 1:17 and 8:1).

Vanity had many questions: "*Does Christ automatically forgive us of everything that we've done when we accept him?*"

Faith told Vanity that while Jesus died for our sins, it is our responsibility to agree with him about our sins by repenting and confessing them by name. There is one sin that the Lord deems unforgivable. Faith turned to the Book of Matthew and began to read: "*Every sin and blasphemy can be forgiven, except blasphemy against the Holy Spirit. Anyone who speaks against the Son of Man can be forgiven, but anyone who speaks against the Holy Spirit will never be forgiven, either in this world or the world to come*" (see Matthew 1:31). Faith went on to explain blasphemy as an act of speaking sacrilegiously (profanely or irreverently) about the Holy Spirit. She told her young friend that God loved her so much that he wanted to forgive her, but she had to ask. Vanity wanted to know how to seek forgiveness for the things that she had done in her past. She wept as she said, "I just didn't know any better!"

Faith opened the Bible again and began to read to her, using excerpts to simplify the scriptures that if she *confessed her sins*, calling them out by name and earnestly express a deep heartfelt sorrow, with the intent of never returning to those sinful practices, the Lord will forgive her (see 1 John 1:9). He will also restore you into right standing with him. In his eyesight, it would be just as if it never happened. Vanity was excited about forgiveness and restoration. But she still had some apprehensions. She blurted out, "*Do I have to confess in front of the pastor, or someone like that?*" Faith assured her that her confession could be between her and the Lord, and with that, Faith asked Vanity if she believed that black magic existed. Vanity said that she truly believed and wondered why no one had ever told her about stuff like that before. Vanity said that she had been in church all her life, and no one ever told her about the things they discussed! Faith told her that that was why it was required of true Christians to study to the Bible for themselves so that they can present themselves to

God and receive his approval. Once this occurs, you can correctly explain the truths revealed in the Bible! Always know that when the pupil is ready to receive the truth, the teacher will come!

Faith told Vanity that to allow herself to momentarily reflect on the behavior of people in high places acting out of character for the positions they held. This might give her a better grasp being *under the influence* of evil compelling forces. Vanity asked, "How can I do that?" Faith answered her on this wise. Give your imagination free range for a moment. Imagine a major political meeting room filled with the presently reigning hierarchal entities of your government. The room in that *House of Governess* might be filled with *intellectually* knowledgeable women and men with all manner of degrees. They're all dressed in designer attire. Each individual's hair is professionally coiffed and nails well-manicured. Those are the men and women that the masses elected to protect the nation's best interest and serve all the citizens of the nation. Seemingly, most of those officials acted in good faith at one time or the other. Gradually, an *opposing* change began to take place, and they began to behave in a way that opposed the laws that they swore to protect and serve. Noticeably, most of them seemed to have drank from the same *amnesiac* fountain and totally forgot how to govern! Without any forewarning, the people for whom they work (the citizens) became secondary to them. Obviously, a majority of the officials are *under the influence* of *evil compelling* forces, and they don't even know it! They seem to be like sheep being led to an idiotic slaughter house. The force that is triggering them to act outside integrity and morality, required for the positions they hold, is the devil. They are *under the influence* of the spirits of greed, self-interest, and lust, among other adverse things. Apparently, they are worshipping a creature versus the Creator.

Vanity asked Faith, "*Why does God allow this type of thing go on?*"

Faith answered thusly, "Knowing God and developing a relationship with him gives way to revelation knowledge about him. Actually, what the world is experiencing now was prophesized long ago as he was teaching his disciples." Faith suggested Vanity read the twelfth chapter of Matthew in its entity where Jesus foretells of his future and things that will happen as the last days approach. Faith read, "*Sin will be rampant everywhere and the love of many will grow cold*" (see Matthew 11). Then she jumped over to 2 Timothy and read, "*In the last days there will be very difficult times. For people will love only themselves…they will consider nothing sacred*" (see 2 Timothy 3:1–3). God gave everyone the right to make decisions for themselves. Some *choose* to follow the ways of the enemy by omission. Therefore, their reigning god is the devil. Others *choose* to follow Christ by devoting themselves to his teachings. They are Christians. Everyone are under the influence of the devil or God!

Contrary to all the propaganda about race, religion, and other social beliefs, there are only two kinds of people in the world: the saved and unsaved! Therefore, people under the enemy's jurisdiction are doing the will of their god. The bad thing about all that is they don't know that they are under the devil's influence. They actually believe that they are doing the right thing. We are not to judge them though. In the fullness of time, God will judge everyone for whatever they did or didn't do, be it good or evil.

Actually, the officials, under the devil's influence, are in bondage to him. They are in direct opposition to the Word of God: "*I will not allow deceivers to serve in my house, and a liar will not stay in my presence says the Lord*" (see Psalm 101:7–8). However, numerous people follow after the deceivers and liars due to their own spiritual blindness.

We are to look at them with disappointment and compassion because large numbers of them are not aware of the public's scrutiny. Many people are only aware of the *tip of the iceberg* regarding the influential power of the devil operating in the world around them. Because of lack of spiritual insight and discernment, dark influential forces might be operating in some of their lives through people and unknown sources as we speak. Through prayer and supplication, most things can be revealed to believers as they study the Word of God. People, invalidating the reality of mental invasion and spiritual hijacking, usually have no authentic knowledge about such things. As a result, they simply *choose* the path of least resistance by denying that an evil divergent entity is actually powerful enough to superimpose his will upon them. Many advances have been made in various areas of life, but many believers, and nonbelievers alike, are still perishing because they lack knowledge.

Faith encouraged Vanity to begin reading her Bible on a regular basis to feed her spirit as well as she fed her body. Faith assured Vanity that once she came to a place where she could totally and completely trust God in all areas of her life, he would further revel himself to her. Revelation knowledge is the spiritual act of hiding the Word in one's heart. This can only be done by the power of the Holy Spirit. Vanity asked Faith if she thought that she could ever become as accomplished in the Word as she, Faith, was.

Faith assured her young friend that she was not the standard by which she should to endeavor to reach. Every individual was born to fulfill a divine purpose. The Lord equips each individual with whatever he needs to fulfill that purpose. Along the way, he might also add other divine missions to believers willing to relinquish control of their lives to him. When a believer allows himself to come *under the influence* of the Holy Spirit, it becomes easy to know and fulfill his divine purpose. Not only does it become easy, it becomes a joy as well! The Holy Spirit will not use force, inducement, or any other means to alter the behavior of anyone. The Holy Spirit recognizes and respects the free will of each individual to make independent choices. Thus, he intervenes by invitation only! Each person must willingly ask him to enter into their lives and living situations. The intentions of the Holy Spirit are *always* in the best interest of the believer. The life of each believer should exist to bring glory, honor, and praise to God!

Free will is God's gift to human beings that allows each individual to make decisions on their own. Even though many human decisions might be wrong, the Lord does not intervene unless the believer asks for his assistance. The indwelling Holy Spirit reminds believers of what is right and wrong and good and evil. But he does not force human beings to do anything. Acceptance of the invitation to ask and it will be given, seek and you will find, and knock and the door will be opened for you means that you relinquish your will to the Lord. That way, he is *not* going against your will to divinely intervene in your life situations. Once he has intervened in any given situation, your will becomes under your control again. But you can repeat the asking, seeking, and knocking as many times as you need to.

Dark and evil spirits are calculatedly constructed by the devil. Evil has no respect for its victims' desires and hopes. Their objectives are always wicked. They use whatever means necessary to capture their prey. All manner of mind-altering substances, omens, and other forms of inducements are used to lead their victims astray.

Vanity asked, "Where do the evil spirits get the power to enter into one's life and take control of their moral fiber?" Faith explained that dark and evil spirits are empowered by the devil, whose power is secondary to God's. Just as the Holy Spirit seeks to do the will of God, the Father, and the Son, evil spirits seek to do the will of their father, the devil. The devil's primary goals are to kill, steal, and destroy. Jesus came to earth in the flesh so that those who believed in him could have a more prosperous spiritual life. This does not necessarily mean a more materially prosperous life. Nevertheless, he's not angry when his children prosper financially. All the needs of believers are met on a daily basis. He wants individuals to keep everything in prospective by putting him first in their lives. This can be done by seeking the kingdom of heaven and *all* the righteousness of God first. Then everything that believer's *need* will be released to them (see Matthew 6:33).

Vanity was amazed at the simplicity at which Faith explained things. She wanted to know what she needed to do with all the knowledge that she was acquiring. Faith told her use it as a guide to making lifestyle changes and share it. Faith suggested beginning with her friend Damiona. Vanity wasn't sure how she could approach Damiona with her newfound wisdom. Faith repeated Vanity's need to trust God for guidance. She also told Vanity to wait upon the guidance from the Holy Spirit before approaching Damiona, or anyone else. Faith left Vanity with this statement: "Always trust the Lord in everything you do. Don't rely on your limited understanding. Ask the Lord for directions *before* making a move and wait in him to direct you" (see Proverbs 3:5)!

# Calculated Crafty Control

There will always be aftereffects of the actions that people choose to take. However, some are not totally aware of the consequences. Calculated proceedings are taken with a thorough understanding of the consequences involved. Everything the enemy does is figured out ahead of time with disparaging implications. He is *crafty* at achieving his own goals by unforeseen, untrustworthy methods. All the enemy's calculating and crafty undertakings are performed to clench the power to *control* the endeavors of human beings.

Generally, calculations are done as a means of judging the success, or failure of a specific process. But as discussions commence within the dark arena of the physical world, calculating is a callous, merciless plan aimed at promoting the devil's ego, his vanity, and display his aversion to humankind. The precise way the enemy calculates his attacks usually assures him of success in his endeavors. But his victories are short-lived in the lives of God's children. Craftiness is a characteristic trait of the enemy, which is used as an instrument to scheme, outwit, and entrap his prey. Control is the enemy's way of systematically exercising absolute influence over everyone under his power. All these tactics are choreographed by the archenemy of God to corrupt the human mind, body, and soul.

Joshua Pruitt was on top of the world. He was rapidly climbing the corporate ladder and seemingly reaching his projected goals at a much faster pace than he had anticipated. Joshua was surrounded by successful friends, lived in a cutting edge condo, and drove a BMW. In a moment's twinkling of the eye, Joshua's life changed for the worst. After years of hard work and self-denial, everything that he had accomplished was diminishing before his very eyes, and he could do nothing to stop the decline!

One bright and sunny day, Joshua was casually driving home from work. He was approaching a green light at a busy intersection. A big delivery truck was approaching the same intersection from the opposite direction. The truck driver dropped his cell phone and bent down to retrieve it. His attention was divided, and he crossed over the dividing line and plowed head on into Joshua's BMW. Joshua gained consciousness about twenty-four hours later in excruciating pain! His parents and other relatives were at his bedside. They quickly summonsed the nurse.

The nurse injected a potent narcotic substance into his vein. The medication took effect almost immediately. The nurse informed Joshua and his family that she was connecting a small bag of fluid to the larger one. The smaller bag had been infused with a potent pain-relieving medication. Whenever Joshua needed to be medicated, he could push the button on the pump through, which fluids ran. However, he could only use the button at four hour intervals. If his pain became unbearable between intervals, they could call for the nurse to inject him with a different painkiller. Whenever Joshua received pain medication, he became so affected until he began to sense the presence of nonexistent mechanisms (i.e., curtains blowing at the windows where here were no curtains).

Not only did the medication take away the pain, but Joshua also received a reprieve from reality. Once he became fully aware of what had happened to him, Joshua welcomed the escape from reality. It didn't take long for Joshua's body to begin craving the powerful narcotics that had modified his mental perception.

The accident had caused Joshua to suffer multiple disabling injuries, including gashes in both of his legs, which had to be treated. He had to remain immobile for several weeks. By the time Joshua was ready to begin the rehabilitation process, his level of pain had decreased tremendously. But the clinical staff had failed to decrease the strength and/or the amount of medication he received.

As a matter of fact, as a result of the rapidity of the addiction of the potent opioids, Joshua's body began to crave more drugs. Again, without any type of titration of the existing drugs, the treating physician added another mind-altering drug to Joshua's list of medications.

Titration is a process whereby the dosage of a medication is adjusted to give patients the best possible benefits without destructive effects, such as addiction. The concept of titration is as the patient heals the *need* for powerful addictive drugs should be decreased incrementally before the patient becomes dependent on the drug. However, the negligent behavior, responsible for addiction to prescribed drugs, is influenced by numerous factors. The most prevalent one being money. The drug manufacturers, along with the prescribing physicians and the dispensing pharmacists, are all a part of a well-crafted plan to induce dependency on expensive drugs. Joshua was not necessarily a targeted victim. He just fell into the category that numerous other people on whom drug manufactures preyed.

At one time, opioids, such a morphine and fentanyl, were used alongside anesthesia for surgical patients. That was when narcotics were regulated by government agents. Prescribing physicians were required, by the agency that oversaw use and dispensing of narcotics, to report numbers of controlled substances prescribed to individual patients. Because the *legal drug dealers'* (pharmaceuticals) gained pre-eminence over government officials via their financial powers, manufacturers were given authority to addict clients at will. Therefore, *legal drug dealers* began to produce more lethal drugs, which caused a more rapid addiction so that the pharmaceutical heirs could amass more wealth. As the *legal drug* industry grew, so did the price of their products! The pharmaceutical industry sets their own prices. The average cost of prescribed opioids is around twenty-two dollars a pill. A thirty-day supply can cost over six hundred dollars. Prescriptions are generally written to cover patients for ninety days. Over forty-five million dollars was amassed by the drug industry from the sale of opioids alone in two thousand and fifteen! That total did not include all other prescribed drugs.

Doctors always knew the effects and side effects of opioids as well as the cost. Drug manufacturers, intentionally, mass produced those dangerous substances for their financial benefit. Their respective companies pay representatives healthy salaries, along with numerous perks, to entice doctors to prescribe opioids. Lucrative incentives are passed on to some doctors who order their products. Together, health-care professionals and drug manufacturers constructed a calculated crafty plan to make sure the industry prospered handsomely at the expense of addicted victims.

Opioid ingestion is the most classic form of being *under the influence* of self-aggrandizing forces controlled by the archenemy of integrity, moral principles, and ethic responsibility. At some point during the course of addiction, many clients begin to turn to *illegal drug* dealers to satisfy their cravings after the prescribing physicians cut them off.

Introducing mind-altering drugs by way of induction, injections, and other widely used methods of *treatment* can have the same effect as demonic spiritual invasion. Anything that alters one's ability to make sound decisions based on truth can impact the overall physical and mental health of a person. The effects of initiating mind-altering substances with the *potential* to change the sensory aspect of a person's mental sharpness are limitless. Health-care professionals and drug producers know that all narcotics are addictive if taken long enough. Yet they freely dispense them to unsuspecting patients without caution or warnings. The drug industry looks for the most lucrative ways possible to fuel their greed. They do this at the expense of innocent people, whose lives they destroy.

Drug addiction is often referred to as *substance abuse disorder* to make the condition less weighty! Once a person becomes addicted, he is declared sick! Now that the addiction to opioids had become extremely widespread, the same industry that created the addictive drugs is *creating other addictive drugs* to combat the effects of the first drug! Well, when one is *under the influence* of a substance, their sensory perceptions are diminished. If that does not make sense to the natural mind, that's probably because the origin of the *power to control* occurs in a spiritual realm. That same craving to gain and maintain control over someone, or something else continues to evolve within the spirit world of darkness. People whose allegiances are to the true Creator of all things know that the entities that they are fighting against are not human in nature. The real enemies are evil rulers and authorities and mighty powers in the dark world and evil spirits in heavenly places (see Ephesians 6–12). It has been said that *power corrupts, and absolute power corrupts absolutely!* The devil is very pleased when he utterly destroys the life of a believer.

Over time, Joshua's body recovered from the accident. However, because of his ravenousness desire to live in the cocoon of drug addiction, his mental and physical condition continued to deteriorate. He lost his job, his condo, and everything else he possessed. The health-care team dismissed him and refused to write him any more prescriptions. He went to the streets to buy drugs.

Before long, well-educated, most-promising bachelor Joshua was recognized by a friend, Jon, sleeping in the hallway of his apartment building. Joshua was unkempt and a total mess! Jon took Joshua to his apartment, allowed him to shower, gave him a change of clothes, and fixed dinner for him. After Joshua had settled in, Jon began to talk to him about life, liberty, and the pursuit of happiness. Joshua told Jon his story. Jon assured Joshua that he didn't have to stay in the shape he was in.

Joshua talked about rehabilitation centers. Jon told him about an instant divine way of healing that could change him immediately. For the first time in months, Joshua seemed to have come awake. He excitedly asked John where and how he could get such a healing! Jon talked to Josh for a few minutes about Jesus and the amazing intense love that he had for him. Joshua was surprised that Jesus still loved him in his wretched state, but he really wanted to return to his life before drugs. So he asked Jon, "What do I have to do?" Jon told him that if he had to believe that Jesus was the Son of God and admit that he was a sinner in need of saving from the wiles of the devil and eternal hell fire. Jon paused to explain that everyone born of the seed of a man was a sinner. Joshua said, "I have no problem acknowledging that I am a sinner man." Then Jon got his Bible, turned to Romans 10:9–10, and asked Joshua to repeat the scripture verses. Joshua repeated, "*If you confess with your mouth that Jesus is Lord, and God raised him from the dead, you will be saved. For it is by believing in your heart that you are made right with God, and it is by confessing with your mouth that you are saved.*" Suddenly, Josh thought that he felt the fuzziness that had been in his head for too long begin to clear. He thanked God and Jon for leading him to his second chance at life.

Jon took his friend by the shoulder and said to him, "Man, I need to pray with you about this *monkey that's on your back.*" Jon promised Josh that he would not send him back out into the world unarmed. He offered Josh a room in his home until he got back on his feet. Not only did Jon follow the Lord's command to *compel* his friend to come to Christ, he also began to *teach him whatever he had been taught.* After a few days of prayer and meditation on the Lord, Josh no longer desired drugs. He became a new creation in Christ Jesus. He had been divinely released from the gripping power of drugs that had controlled his being for much too long.

Josh gained God-ordained strength. He recognized that he had given up his power to the drugs that had controlled his life. Josh not only accepted the gift of redemption, he became a witness who began sharing the Word.

# The Power to Control

Multitudes of children gathered around the stage of an auditorium to see a puppet show. Puppeteers, the actual people controlling the puppets, were met with excited applause from the crowd. Once the children became engrossed in the show, they were not aware of the fact that the puppeteers were the ones pulling strings to move various parts of the puppet's body. The puppeteers mad it *look like* the inanimate puppets were talking, but they used their own voices to speak for the puppet. In reality, the puppets were just lifeless objects used to mystify and entertain the children. The puppeteers used his power to totally control the puppets movements.

Power has numerous connotations, depending on what it's used for and how it's used. Power enables entities to wield force and to exercise influence over people and situations exclusive of being in charge officially. Power is indicative of being in possession of someone or something with the authority to control that which he possesses. In some instances, power means to supply with the energy to perform.

Mortal beings' inherent desire for power is built into their *natural* nature inherited from Satan. It was the spirit of Satan embedded within a serpent that deceived Adam and Eve in the garden. His natural inclination was to acquire enough power to control anything that belonged to God. When the couple ate the forbidden fruit, their pure, uncorrupted nature changed (died), and the *nature* of the Satan replaced their godly nature. From that day forward, the natural nature of humanity is perceived as the seat of corruption. Therefore, when Jesus underwent everything necessary for redemption, the old corrupt nature did not change. A new more powerful nature was ushered in, which was the Holy Spirit of Jesus Christ. The enemy has consistently endeavored to use his power to influence humanity to follow the dictates of the flesh rather than the influence of the Spirit. "*The sinful nature wants to do evil, which is just the opposite of what the spiritual nature wants. And the spirit gives us desires that are the opposite of what the sinful nature desires. Those two forces are constantly fighting each other… Those who belong to Christ Jesus have nailed the passions and desires of their sinful nature and crucified them there to the cross*" (see Galatians 5:17 and 24). The enemy uses his power to keep the desire of the old nature alive within the minds of believers who have been redeemed.

Mortal beings, under the influence of the enemy, can be likened to a puppet, and the devil (puppeteer) controlling their characters and overall dispositions. Lucifer coveted the power of God and was said to have strived to overthrow God so that he could have all that power! Many a battle has ensued over the power to control others in all areas of life. We witness it in political arenas where the objective is not governing but rather the opportunity to *be in charge*. Human beings have a natural desire for power, of which no amount will ever be enough. That *inherent* desire can be compared to a consuming fire, always clamoring for more logs to keep it going; otherwise, it would just turn to ashes and eventually cease to be a fire.

The power to control is still the central goal of the enemy. Since he is a spirit, without a physical body, he tries to implant his spirit within the bodies of whatever or whomever is available to him. He knows that he has already lost the battle against God. So in order *to get back at God*, he targets God's most beloved creatures—human beings. He searches for human frailties and *exposed* vulnerabilities to gain access to the power to control them. His evil game plan is to undermine God's goals for his people.

Once upon a time, a child, Rudy Blitzkrieg, was born into a middle-class family in Old Havilland on the outskirts of a wealthy upper-class neighborhood. The Blitzkrieg family had emigrated to Old Havilland from a poor neighborhood in Europe. Rudy was the third of three children. He absolutely detested his family's status in life because of their background. Rudy hated being called an immigrant because of the unacceptable implication of not belonging. For that reason, Rudy made a decision when he was quite young to amass great wealth and climb the social ladder at any cost. Then people would fear him because he would become powerful enough to look down on those who looked down on him.

Rudy's anger emanated from the innermost sanctum of his being. When his plans were not coming together fast enough, he sought out a notorious gang leader in a neighboring community, dubbed Beastow. He was intrigued with the power the gang leader wielded over members of his gang as well as the fear his presence engendered. Rudy was not particularly interested in joining the gang that he had observed. Nevertheless, being on a *whatever-it-takes* mission to reach his goal, he joined the gang for the sole purpose of learning what it took to become powerful enough to exert control over others. After a few months, Rudy was introduces to the leader.

Rudy's middle-class status gave him easy access to *money-spinning* information. Beastow's goals were similar to Rudy's, but the two young adults employed different approaches to achieving their goals. Wealth was at the apex of both men's designs. Each had something of value to bring to the table that the other needed.

Rudy's educational background and acquired social status placed him in the presence of wealthy executives of thriving companies. Beastow had the power to control the courses of the lives of his underlings and others who knew him. Together, they calculatingly crafted a plan to merge their strong suits so that each man could achieve his goals more rapidly. Rudy promised to pass along profitable financial data that he had accrued along the way. He also promised to introduce Beastow to businessmen whom he wanted to rip off. In exchange, Beastow shared bullying and blustering tactics that could empower Rudy in the public's eye with the promise to avail his toughest gang members to him whenever he needed *reinforcement.* Thus, enhancing Rudy's abilities to gain and maintain the power to control other people around him.

Rudy and Beastow did not have a friendship type of relationship. Each was using the other to boost their status. Neither of them trusted the other. Neither of them had any inkling what it meant to love anyone outside themselves. They both detested taking orders from anyone else, and both of them ravenously sought enough power to be in control. They both wanted people to look up to them.

Rudy didn't care much for school, but his ancestors insisted that he become educated, or at least get a degree. A degree represented respectability for the Blitzkrieg clan. Because some of his ancestors had become wealthy, they put forth every effort to make financial contributions to Rudy's education. His family sought, and were granted, special favors from educational institutions on Rudy's behalf for a fee. So Rudy obtained degrees that he didn't earn. Upon graduating from college, Rudy was almost unenlightened and unsophisticated. But he had used his bullying and intimidating skills to enter into some productive business deals with wealthy professionals. His family insisted on Rudy learning proper social skills that would serve him well if he wanted to mingle among the city's *elite* groups.

By the time Rudy reached twenty-five, he had attained name recognition as a wealthy software tycoon. He fabricated information regarding his assets to obtain substantial bank loans. When he failed to pay according to the contractual agreement, he publicly loud-mouthed the lending institutions and oftentimes threatened to sue them for slander. Rudy protested bitterly and publicly, saying that the institution's contracts were misleading, if not fraudulent. Rudy even got some of his renegade associates to alter his copy of contracts to reflect something different from the lending institution's contracts. Oftentimes, lending institutions in question would write off the loans and quietly go away. However, this practice adversely affected his ability to do business with most lending institutions.

Rudy's old friend, Beastow, contacted him with a new deal. The deal would be very rewarding for the both of them, but it involved a number of shady negotiations. Beastow needed Rudy's social status to gain access into the inner circles of prosperous conglomerates. Since Beastow was a bit rough around the edges, Rudy hired a life coach to teach him some important points of decorum regarding style of dress and communication techniques. He explained that most of the owners and controllers of the businesses that he came in contact with had been just like them at some time in their lives. Most of them were living a lie and putting on airs to impress each other. If they wanted to play the game, they had to *artistically* fit in the circles of the rich and famous. Some of *those people* inflated their assets and minimized their liabilities. They all had underlings to do their biddings. But the assets of companies they were associated with were sound. They decided to change Beastow's name to a more respectable name: B. Ellington.

Once *B. Ellington* became more familiar as someone with equal social and financial status within the inner circles, he quickly secured their confidence. With a few key words and bits and pieces of information, *B. Ellington* had underlings who could retrieve enough information to gain access into the financial assets of numerous well-known companies. Beastow had many talented underlings within his gang. He used some of his tech-savvy gang members to electronically embezzle large sums of money from various corporations over a period of time. He shared portions of the bounty with Rudy but not the tactics used to amass the large sums of money. He and Rudy made a pact to never mention each other in their dealings. Beastow had sold his soul to the devil long before he met Rudy. He made all kinds of claims about a relationship with god. His god was indeed the prince of the dark world. The more familiar Rudy became with Beastow, the more he admired him.

Rudy's family were *religious,* but they chose to worship their gods in their own way. Because achievements were placed above love within Rudy's family, he was more familiar with revulsion than he was with love. His animosity motivated him to seek enough power to control his family and everyone else who criticized him.

Rudy eventually became extremely wealthy by any means necessary. But he was too occupied with always being on top to actually enjoy his wealth. He had no idea that he was *under the influence* of evil spirits. He had no idea of their existence! He was willing to try anything that could provide him with the ability to influence the behavior of others and change the course of events in their lives. Rudy became a consummate liar about anything and everything, just like his father, the devil. He became a thief, just like his father, the devil. Rudy became a murderer, just like his father, the devil. He did not exactly verbally denounce God. But his characteristic traits revealed the evil spirit to whom he was loyal.

Rudy consciously *chose* the *broad and wide road* that leads to destruction. He had an unquenchable desire for beautiful women, and his wealth and social status, along with his good looks and opulent lifestyle, were magnets that attracted such women. He used, then abused them and discarded them with the threat of death if they ever disclosed anything personal about him. The one female who attempted to publicly shame him was met with slander as well as a violent visit from assailants from Beastow's gang. That woman's lifestyle was made public, which served notice to all other female associates of Rudy.

Rudy was like many other stiff-necked people who believed that they were the captains of their souls. As a young boy, he had gone to church with some of his friends and learned about God. He *knew the truth about God because he (God) had made it obvious to him. But he would not worship him.* God abandoned Rudy *to do whatever his shameful heart desired.* As a result, Rudy began to think up foolish ideas of what God was like. His mind became dark and confused. He made ranting proclamations about how smart he was. But instead, he was labeled as foolish. God *gave him over to a degenerate mind* (see Ro. 1:24–28). Rudy began to believe his lies, and he was granted power, by the ruler of this dark world, to gain entry into the minds of others by way of propaganda and brainwashing tactics. In essence, unknowingly, Rudy became one of the devil's servants. He believed that the world's acceptance of his lies, deceptions, and other schemes were proof of his wisdom and knowledge. However, more than a few people saw him as a dimwitted, unenlightened thug.

When someone is under the influence of a dark spirit, they are oblivious to their unsavory behavior. This is in total opposition to the Word, which says, "*Trust the Lord with all your heart; do not depend on your own understanding. Seek His will in all you* do and He will tell you which path to take" (see Proverbs 3:5–6).

There is only one road that leads to freedom and deliverance. That is that straight and *narrow road* with a narrow gate leading to Jesus Christ. On that road, the gate is so narrow that only one person can pass through at a time. The journey that one must travel to enter in through the narrow gate was mapped out by the Creator of humankind. Everyone is given a choice as to which road he chooses to travel. That gate is Jesus, through which one must pass to enter into an eternity with the Lord. Each entrant's journey is personal. Each person will be rewarded in accordance to the choices that he made.

Numerous people, like Vanity, did not believe the reality that one entity had the ability to take authority over the behavior of someone else, or even direct the course of events for the benefit of the manipulator. But actually, the practice of mind control is as old as time. The one thing to remember is that there is an organized framework within the adversary's domain aimed at that one fact. The powers of the evil ruling spirits are mighty. Evil spirits are forever traveling through the earthly domain, looking for victims to consume, demolish, and engulf. Those demonic spirits are assigned to overwhelm human beings by taking control of their minds, their approaches to life, and their temperaments, and they have enough power to do so too.

Just as Jesus stands at the door of unbeliever's hearts knocking and waiting to be invited in, the devil is standing right there as well. The difference is the devil is not polite enough to wait for an invitation. He just forces his way into the minds of people and steer them into darkness. The demons are duty bound to fulfill the purpose of their father, the devil, which is to kill, steal, and destroy! Therefore, access into a person's mind by seducing spirits does not necessarily depend on his belief, or disbelief in their existence. As a matter of fact, they quickly pounce on those who do not believe that they exist. Realistic information is still real, even if no one believes it!

The decision to execute domination over others, or shape public opinion regarding good and evil and right or wrong, is an attempt to take God's sovereign place of authority. The governmental systems in place today show leaders in authoritative positions attempting to exercise absolute power over others regularly. Absolute power belongs to God alone!

As we approach a different phase of life within the earth, wickedness *seems* to reign, and the devil's cause *seems* to be gaining. But remember this. While the enemy is powerful, his power is secondary to God's power. When his lease to have dominion over the worldly domain expires, he and all his demons will be dealt a final blow. They, along with their followers, will be tossed into the pit of hell for all eternity. There are people who contradict the reality of hell. Some have even attempted to soften its meaning to hades. Nevertheless, that does not affect its existence as a realistic place.

Unbelief is a wide open door that leads to the devil's domain. It's like an embossed invitation for him to invade the human mind. He has numerous tactics in his arsenal. He uses them over and over again in unsuspecting people. His objective is to slide into the psyche of human beings unnoticed.

All his schemes and tactics are as old as time. King Solomon asserted: "*History merely repeats itself. It has all been done before. Nothing under the sun is truly new*" (see Ecclesiastes 1:9). So as we delve into some of the evil practices of old, remember the devil uses the same ones over and over again because they work for him.

# Witchcraft and Casting Spells

When most people think about witchcraft, the animation of a hideous creature with a long nose, wearing a black hat, bending over a pot brewing repugnant portions, comes to mind. That distorted simulation makes witchcraft and the casting of spells seem like a harmless cartoon. Nothing could be further from the truth. Well-dressed scholarly people with highly respected professional positions can also be workers of iniquity on behalf of the devil. The devil has servants everywhere, even in churches, pulpits, choir stands, and in the pews. Jude warned believers about such people: *"Some ungodly people have wormed their way into your churches, saying that God's marvelous grace allows us to live immoral lives. The condemnation of such people was recorded long ago…m"* (see Jude 4–5).

Witchcraft and the casting of spells is not child's play as the deceiver of mankind would like for you to believe. It involves serious offenses aimed at demon possession and supreme authority over as many people as possible. If you close your eyes, it won't go away.

Demon possession is exactly what it says it is: being overcome, controlled, and owned, to some degree, by demon spirits. Some implied symptoms of demon possession include memory lapses, loss of the sense of self-control, and distorted awareness to name a few. But the Spirit of the Living God is powerful enough to cast the demons out. He gave his disciples authority to cast out evil spirits in his name (see Matthew 20:1). Jesus even healed those possessed with demon spirits. *"Whatever sickness, or disease, or if they were demon-possessed, Jesus healed them all"* (see Matthew 8:16).

Angel Blue was not as physically attractive as her older sister, Cherub, and her younger sister, Seraph. Angel was thin and unshapely. She had buckteeth and slightly curly hair that did not flow like that of her sisters'. She loved and admired both of her sisters and wished that she could be more like them. But they ruthlessly teased her about her teeth and the lack of a good physique. Angel took all their ribbing in stride, pretending that she was not hurt by their spiteful words. One day, Angel was talking with an older female neighbor, Mrs. Zen, about her sisters and how bad they made her feel inside.

Angel felt safe with Mrs. Zen because she believed that they had something in common. Mrs. Zen's house was dark and musty, and she rarely had any visitors during the day. So she relished Angel's brief visits. Angel didn't have many friends either. On the day in question, Mrs. Zen looked at Angel, who was about nine at the time, with a twinkle in her eyes and a naughty smile on her face. She asked Angel if she wanted to learn how to *cast a spell* on her sisters so that they would not tease her anymore. Angel pondered the thought in her mind for a moment before asking, "What's a spell?" Mrs. Zen told her it was like a magic trick that required her to do some things that she had probably never done before. But she assured her young friend that the *magic trick* would work.

Suddenly, Angel became afraid, and she didn't know why. She jumped up from the couch and ran out of Mrs. Zen's house, looking like she had seen a ghost!

Angel couldn't wait for her mother, Mrs. Alpha Blue, to come home so that she could talk with her about Mrs. Zen and magic spells! It seemed like forever before Angel's mother came home. But finally, Angel heard her mother's voice, and she rushed to meet her. She began to rapidly fire questions at her mother such as "Momma, what is a magic spell? Can people cast spells on someone to make them stop doing something they don't like?" Angel's mother saw the fear and confusion in her child's eyes. So she sat right down and asked Angel, "Why are you asking about spells?" Angel recounted her conversation with Mrs. Zen.

Mrs. Blue took a moment to think before answering Angel. She and some of the neighbors had long believed that Mrs. Zen dabbled in occultism. Occultism involves paranormal experiences, which are said to be satanic in nature. It is believed that those who practice spell casting are empowered by some sort of evil-spirited agent.

Following a prolonged silence, Mrs. Blue told Angel that she must never go to Mrs. Zen's house without someone with her because people were saying that what Mrs. Zen called magic was really a terrible thing! Therefore, I don't want you to get mixed up in anything bad.

The Blue family were practicing Christians, and they had taught Angel and her sisters about Jesus and a little bit about the devil. Mrs. Blue knew that it was time to teach angel a little about the dark spiritual world that operated within the earth. She knew that Satan preyed on the minds of the young as well as other innocent, unsuspecting people. She also knew that Mrs. Zen was doing what people influenced by the devil does. The Bible says that Christians should use whatever special abilities that the Spirit of God gives them to bring glory to God (see 1 Corinthians 14:1). The devil (in Revelations 12 and 13) also commands his demons to seek people with special abilities to serve him. He wants to use God-given abilities for his purposes as well as oppose God's purpose and plan.

God granted Satan enough power to do *some* things for a limited time and with his permission. Satan, seen as the dragon in Revelations, finally received something he'd always wanted—to be worshiped for giving the beast's great power.

Mrs. Blue knew that she had to find a simple way to tell Angel about all those things without inciting fear. Therefore, she made up a simple little fairytale about lambs, dragons, and beast, centering the principles on Angel and her two sisters, Cherub and Seraph. She decided to include a pseudonym of Mrs. Zen in the narrative as well. Here's Mrs. Blue's storyline:

Once upon a time, in the magical city of Crystals, there lived an old woman called Sage. Sage had always lived in the same house with running vines that grew along a wood-framed trellis that went from the ground upward until the plants reached top of her roof. The vines prevented anyone from seeing onto her porch. They also prevented sunlight from entering into her house from the front.

Therefore, Mrs. Sage's house was always dark and had a stuffy smell. It was rumored that Mrs. Sage practice a different non-Christ-centered religion from that of her neighbors.

Mrs. Sage was pleasant enough, but the neighbors avoided her. She was married to a tall handsome gentleman who rarely spoke and obeyed Mrs. Sage in a childlike manner. It was rumored that Mrs. Sage had *cast a spell* on him, which gave her the power to control his behavior.

On more than a few occasions, a small group of women were seen leaving Mrs. Sage's house before dawn, dressed in all black outfits with their faces concealed beneath black see-through veils. It was rumored that Mrs. Sage and her friends practiced new ways to cast spells on people. Mrs. Blue told her girls that it was also rumored that Mrs. Sage was deeply involved in issues associated with the spiritual world of darkness. Magic spells have lots of different names, such as sorcery, occultism, conjuring, incantations, and divinations. All those terms are associated with black magic. They differ only in how they are used. For example, *sorcery* is the belief in witchcraft, which uses alien power to influence other people. *Occultism* is a belief in and study of deviant powers to bring their subjects under human control. *Divination* is the practice of looking for knowledge of the future by some hazy ungodly means. *Incantation* is a (dark) spiritualist formula used to trigger a hypnotizing effect on a person.

So Mrs. Blue shared this with Angel: "If you allow anyone to convince you that you should use *unknown* powers on people to get them to do what you want them to do, you will become a servant of the devil!" She said to Cherub and Seraph, "To tease someone about the way she look is just as bad as trying to cast a spell on them. All these thoughts and ideas are placed in people's mind by one of the devil's servants. Everyone was created special with very special features that please God. No one is perfect. Therefore, begin to look for the good in each other and complement each other more than you belittle each other. That's how you show love." The girls were very pleased with their mother's story. She had instilled the fear of God in them regarding magic spells.

Mrs. Blue's husband was listening as she talked to the girls. He asked his wife, "What was that all about?" Mrs. Blue told him about Angel's encounter with Mrs. Zen. That left Mr. Blue wondering how she knew all this. Instead of asking her outright, he asked if she knew the theory behind witchcraft. Mrs. Blue began thusly, "The premise, on which witchcraft is based, is founded on Old Testament laws within the Bible. Witchcraft was always evil and was always connected to the devil. Witchcraft and other means of casting spells were also linked to the proverbial conflict between good and evil. Participators in divinations and spell casting usually consider themselves mediators between earthly and spiritual worlds. Often time, they called themselves divine or spiritual healers and prey on weak and unassuming humans who did not know or trust God as a healer. But God used prophets as intermediaries when he had messages for his people before Jesus became the ultimate intermediary. Therefore, those participants of evil, who communicate within the dark spirit worlds, were not from God. There is a term—*necromancy*—that deals directly with the ancient practice of conjuring up the spirits of the dead. Pseudoprophets consult spirits of the dead for the purpose of fortune-telling and giving prediction of the future. Since the enemy of God attempts to bring people *under his influence*, they try to mimic everything that God does. They use necromancy is associated with impersonation of true messengers of the *living* God.

Mrs. Blue noticed her husband's expressions as she was talking to him. She assured him that not everyone was able to readily understand the rationale behind newfound knowledge of the nature she provided, especially after they only given such things a simplistic valuation. She expressed the benefits of studying the Bible and not just reading scriptures. Many things in the Bible must be believed by faith. When the time is right, and the believer is ready, the Spirit will reveal to him as much as he is capable of processing and integrating into his life. She shared this with her husband, *"In my estimation, one of the most lethal outcomes of all the dark powers is the adversary's power to build strongholds within the minds of people."* She ended with "Another subject for another time."

# Concepts of Strongholds

A stronghold is a distinctly fortified environment created to safe-guard whatever or whomever is within its confines. Strongholds are usually designed for the defense of a territory in warfare. In some instances, armed guards are posted within and without a walled fortresses as secondary defenders. Spiritual strongholds are erected in like manner, except they are invisible. Spiritual strongholds are built by the devil for the purpose of detaining those whom they have enticed.

Strongholds are built during a war. The war erected within human minds are crafted to secure the devil's hold on victims so that they will not be set free by the truth regarding Jesus and salvation. His warriors are well-equipped with as much vindictiveness as they need to perform their assignments. No one can easily escape from his fortress because he has legions of demons constantly keeping watch over the souls under his influence. Literally, a legion is about six thousand in number, and the devil is constantly recruiting soldiers to fight on his behalf. But it is not impossible to escape. A stronger spiritual entity is the only entity powerful enough to set prisoners free from the devil's strongholds.

The Lord uses his mighty unequalled power to rescue anyone willing to accept the freedom that he has to offer. "*The Lord is a shelter for the oppressed, a refuge in times of trouble… He does not ignore the cries of those who suffer*" (see Psalms 9:9 and 12). On many occasions, we see the psalmist crying out to the Lord, which is more than a timid whimper.

Unfortunately, those entrapped in the gloomy fortresses of the devil are blinded to the fact that they are in darkness, yet they stumble around through life like drunk men without ever having ingested a drop of alcohol. The devil plays by his own rules and looks for careless unguarded people to pounce on. He even preys on people in their sleep.

Enchanted, a committed servant of the Lord got so involved in her daily activities one day until she fell into bed with praying. She fell fast asleep almost immediately. The enemy was at her bedside waiting for her to enter into a semiconscious state. Once he was certain that the light sleep phase had ended and Enchanted was in a deeper sleep phase, he sent his demons in occupy her mind. He knew just when her brain became de-sensitized or somewhat numbed and the demons rushed in and rapidly began to feed her semi-conscious brain with propaganda. In a semiconscious state, the brain is half asleep and half awake. Remember, the brain does not make distinctions between right and wrong. It responds to inducements that come from the senses. The demons were probably whispering ungodly things in her ears. While in a semiconscious state, her brain and senses might not have been corresponding in a coordinating fashion. The devil was counting on that. But the Holy Spirit was alive and awake.

Enchanted became aware of a harmful presence, but she was not in a position to fight against it. She began to thrash around in their sleep and even made some illegible sounds. She could hear herself and feel the pressure of a force preventing her from getting up. She thrashed around for what seemed like forever. Somewhere in a distance, she clearly heard the Holy Spirit whispering. *"Call out the name of Jesus!"* She tried a few times before she became fully awaken by her own voice shouting Jesus! Once she *cried out to Jesus,* the demons fled, and Jesus rescued her. That is why believers are warned to pray without ceasing (see 1 Thessalonians 5:17). The importance of staying alert and watching out for the great enemy, the devil, is of critical significance. He is always on the prowl, inflating his power and looking for someone to devour (see 1 Peter 5:8).

Many times, tranquility can be mistaken for weakness when one is not observant and vigilant concerning the enemy's snares. The devil is always looking for prime spots to erect a new stronghold, like a developer looks for prime property to build new communities. Many mortal beings glide through life, thinking that they are okay because they deem themselves to be good people but not necessarily godly people. The devil sees such beings as prime property to build new strongholds.

Adam Wisdom was a gentle soul who always looked for the good in people. His tranquil composure was often mistaken for weakness. But deep down within his soul, Abel always *thought* that he knew who he was. He prided himself in being the levelheaded one in a crowd, never engaging in vain disagreements about trivial issues. The adversary assumed that Abel's mannerism made him easy prey. Which, in a sense, it did.

Abel was an average-looking male in his midthirties. He was single and rarely dated, but he stood out in a crowd because he was always impeccably dressed and well-spoken. He had just gotten a promotion on his job from accountant to CFO of a thriving company. Abel was thoroughly surprised but pleased when an attractive young lady, Jezebella (JJ), began to openly seek his attention. Having very little personal interaction with females on an interpersonal level, Abel missed all the *red flags* signifying *danger* when JJ shamelessly came on to him. In a moment's twinkling of the eye, Abel found himself totally out of character whenever he was around JJ. Once JJ convinced Abel that she loved him, he became totally spellbound. She cunningly began to "*make him over*" from the inside out.

JJ did a wardrobe change for him, from tastefully tailored to trendy and flashy. Together, they frequently places that Abel had felt uncomfortable in before JJ. He dropped his old friends and visited his family less and less. He was not aware of the isolation process taking place.

Abel's friends and family began to notice the drastic changes in his demeanor as well as his dress! When his mother, Mrs. Wisdom, asked him what was happening to him, he became angry, so out of character for him! Out of genuine concern for her son, Mrs. Wisdom consulted her pastor, Reverend Baylor, about Abel's behavior. She told the reverend that she noticed a gradual negative change in Abel's behavior a few months after he began dating a beautiful young lady who called herself JJ.

"At first, Abel brought JJ around the family. She was dressed scanty and had a loose tongue. She seemed terribly possessive of Abel and seemingly made sure that she draped her body all over Abel whenever possible. Abel seemed helpless as he uncomfortably fidgeted and looked away from me," his mother shared with the pastor. "However, JJ looked directly at me with a wicked glow in her eyes! She boldly told me that she intended to marry Abel within the next few months! Abel said noting. He didn't seem at all happy, but it was like he was under some kind of spell."

Reverend Baylor asked Mrs. Wisdom if she was familiar with demonic strongholds. With a strange look on her face, she asked, "What do strongholds have to do with my son? Anyway, what is a stronghold?" Noticing Mrs. Wisdom's discomfort with the subject, Reverend decided to begin the discussion by praying with her first to calm her down and solicit some divine intervention. Once peace settled over the room like a cloud, Reverend Baylor began by reminding Mrs. Wisdom of two very familiar biblical metaphors of the Lord as well as the apostle Paul. He reminded her of the principle of sowing and reaping as well as other parables regarding farming and things of that nature. Then the reverend told her that she should be aware of the legendary battle between good and evil, which everyone active participates in by virtue of their human categorization.

Reverend Baylor talked about armies and fortresses built in times of war as measures of security. He went on to say, "Well, people were known to build fortresses to protect the people within the encampments and prevent others from coming into the camps. Those fortresses became known as strongholds. First, a foundation, on which strongholds are to be built, must be laid. Then the *substances* used to *construct* the *defensive walls* are carefully assembled. The expectation is strongholds will keep anyone from entering their confines as well as keeping those within entrenched within from getting out."

Mrs. Wisdom was becoming agitated with the reverend's talk about strongholds. She interrupted the pastor and asked, *"Is any of this going to help my boy?"*

"Oh," the pastor said, "I believe that the young lady in question has a seducing spirit. I believe that she is being controlled by the devil himself. From what you've told me, Abel is, unknowingly, being controlled by an evil spirit. I wanted to paint a picture of what a stronghold is before telling you how it is used in the devil's domain.

"Whenever someone is being held captive by a *demonic* spirit, the devil immediately begins to build strongholds within their minds. His goal is to gain power over their thoughts and cleverly weave his thoughts into his victim's lifestyle. The demonic spirits are persistent and unrelenting. The substance JJ used to build a stronghold depends on her purpose for ensnaring him. We can conclude that she was successful because everyone around him, except him, can see the changes in his behavior. That is one of the first orders of the devil: to blind victims to the truth. The fortification mechanism usually involves *isolation* from godly views and godly people. This can be done by way of seduction, witchcraft, spell casting, or any of the *dark arts.*"

The reverend reminded Mrs. Wisdom of how gentle and kind and faithful Abel had always been until he met JJ. He made it clear that he was not saying that JJ was totally responsible for Abel's progressively negative demeanor. The origin of all dark spiritual strongholds is the devil. The devil uses whatever tools available to him to devastate the character of a light bearer, such as Abel. He deprives unassuming souls of their peaceful attitudes and attempts to damage their character. Perhaps JJ was merely an instrument, or even a disciple of the devil. But she showed signs of possessing a Jezebel (sensual, seducing) spirit. The ability to resist suggestive, sensual seduction is a weakness that too many men, from all walks of life, can't always resist. The inability to resist the attention of an adulterated female is more prevalent in unadulterated males like Abel. The attention seems to hypnotize them, preventing them from seeing beyond their physical desires.

The enemy's disciples use whatever sources available to them to guide their victim into an inappropriate state of mind. In Abel's case, seduction seemed to have been the foundation on which JJ began to build her stronghold. Abel seemed to have bought into JJ's enticing schemes, which brought him under the influence of the enemy. Once the fundamentals of a stronghold are in progress, it's exceptionally challenging for victims to discontinue their downward spiral without divine intervention.

Mrs. Wisdom asked, "Is Abel's situation hopeless? He won't even talk to me anymore without arguing. It seems like I've become his enemy!" Reverend Baylor quickly answered her, saying, "No! No! Do you remember the scripture that says, *The earnest prayers of a righteous person had great power and produces wonderful results* (see James. 5:16)? In his mind, you are his enemy. You see, the enemy that's operating within Abel's mind has the ability to see the Christ in you. It is not you personally that the enemy objects to. It's the Christ within you that he perceives as a *trespasser* trying to enter into the stronghold that he is building within Abel.

"People under the influence of dark forces don't realize that they are being controlled. The enemy wants you to believe that Abel is hopeless so that you will give up on him. But instead, we are going to entreat the Lord on his behalf."

Mrs. Wisdom nodded and asked the pastor if he would stand in agreement with her as *she* prayed for the deliverance of her son. She knew the value of intercessory prayer. Mrs. Wisdom intended to intercede in prayer for Abel's deliverance by clutching God's will until he answered her prayer. While she knew very little about the enemy, she was very familiar with God.

The enemy's objective for building strongholds are consistent with his character. The primary reason many peoples' minds become fertile soil for the enemy to build strongholds include skepticism regarding the reality of strongholds, mental and spiritual disbelief that another person has the power to influence them. Skepticism, disbelief, and *distrust* in God's perfect plan and perfect will are usually the foundation on which strongholds are built.

Each brick thereafter is attached to methods used to further influence victims.

Oftentimes, unfavorable issues arise when believers attempt to convince those in whom the enemy is building strongholds that the enemy has enough power to energize his demons. One of the devil's lies is witchcraft and the likes won't work on anyone who doesn't believe in such nonsense. Before trying to convince someone of the existence of demons and their abilities, pray for guidance from the Holy Spirit. *Wait* on an answer before proceeding further.

Earlier on, mention was made of the dragon, who is a representation of the devil. He gave power to the beast to perform signs and wonders. In Revelations 12:9, the great dragon is referred to as the ancient serpent, the devil, or Satan. These are things that the devil does not want people to believe. No one is exempt from his menacing tactics. Ways to avoid being caught in his snare, as well as obtain deliverance from his control, will be discussed in the last chapter of this script. Believers, *who know the truth found in the inspired Word of God,* are empowered by God. "Jesus said, '*I saw Satan fall from heaven like lightning. Look, I have given you authority over all the power of the enemy'*" (see Luke 10:18–19). When believers *fail* to use their God-ordained power they relinquish it to the devil. Never, never, never give up your power.

Those with spiritual eyes and ears are aware of the vice grip that the devil has on his victims. But the victims are blind and deaf to the hostile actions and routines produced by being under the influence. The devil's guards are fervent in their duties. They form a great wall around the minds of their prey, thus, trying to prevent the light of the Spirit from entering. Believers *must only use the divine power of God* to knock down strongholds. The premise is to use God's weapons versus worldly weapons. Those entrenched within the walls of strongholds use human reasoning and false arguments to justify their ungodly activities. In order for saints to demolish strongholds, they must first destroy every proud obstacle that keeps victims from knowing God. Then they must capture their own rebellious thoughts and teach them to obey Christ (see 2 Corinthians 10:1–5). "*Stand on the promise that the Lord will be shelter for the oppressed and He will be their refuge in times of trouble"* (see Psalm 9:9). Always know that, without Christ Jesus, you can do nothing. But you *"can do all things through Christ who gives you strength"* (see Philippians 4:13).

God can, and will, grant believers of his choosing to assist in demolishing strongholds. The Apostle Paul was granted power to perform many unusual miracles *under the power of God.* A group of men saw Paul performing miracles. They wanted to do likewise without the anointing. They went into the house of a man with an evil spirit. Attempting to drive the evil spirits out, they used the name of Jesus as well as Paul's name in their incantations (spells and charms). The man with the evil spirit said that he knew of Jesus and Paul but not this man. He leaped on the men and attacked them with such violence until they left the house battered and naked (see Acts 19:13–16).

Since believers are not fighting against flesh and blood but, rather, against spiritual forces of darkness in high places, they should continuously prepare themselves for battle. This is done by dressing for success in the full armor of God: *"The belt of truth the body armor of God's* righteousness. *For shoes put on the peace that comes from the Good News so that you will be fully prepared. In addition to all of these, hold up the shield of faith of to stop the fiery arrows of the devil. Put on salvation as your helmet and the sword of the Spirit which is the Word of God"* (see Ephesians 6:11–16). Believers, who have not totally surrendered themselves to the Lord, are in jeopardy of being influenced by Satan.

# Mediums, Methods, and Means

Mediums are people who engage in negotiating, initiating, and transmitting messages between the living and the dead. They refer to themselves spiritual mediums. A more contemporary way for addressing the process is channeling, or even psychic medium. The overall practice embodies controlling, directing, and conducting sessions by a practitioner. There are certain processes or *methods* involved in channeling. Each one is aimed at achieving specific goals. Séances and creating a sense of vagueness or stupor are some of the means mediums employ to enhance the success of their processes. Means characterizes the nature and scope of their methods. The methods and means practiced by mediums are closely associated with occultism. Anxious, desperate people often consult mediums for reasons not associated with calling up sprits of the dead. Some people use mediums to intervene in situations over which they have no plausible control.

The name Ashworth was well-known throughout Alexandro's native land of Stratton. They were among the wealthiest families in the world. Male descendants within that family were rare. All the Ashworth males of child-bearing age, except Alexandro Ashworth, were deceased. Other offspring in the family were females. Alesha's, Alexandro's (Alex) wife, child-bearing years were rapidly coming to a close. She had given birth to three girls and was entering into a critical age where bearing another child could affect her health. She had tried many times to bring forth a male child to keep the Ashworth name alive. However, after three miscarriages, Alesha was not willing to put her body and mind through another attempt.

The family was unreasoningly pressuring Alex to get his wife to try one more time with the promise that *"this will be the last time."* Alesha gave in. After becoming pregnant for the seventh time, her doctor placed her on bed rest, and she had servants to attend to her needs. After about three months, Alesha and Alex learned that she was carrying a male child. They chose not to tell the family until Alesha was at least six months along. Everyone was waiting with bated breath, on a day-by-day basis, for this pregnancy to remain intact.

At the end of her pregnancy, Alesha gave birth to a healthy baby boy. The family named him Andreev (Andy), and a week-long celebration followed the homecoming of mother and son! Andy was the apple of his entire family's eyes. As he grew in statue and knowledge, he learned that the responsibility of keeping the family's name alive was on his shoulders. His family sent him to an international educational institute early on to acclimate him to other cultures.

As Andy became more independent, he wanted to be like all his friends from various parts of the world. Because of his family's expectations, he was not allowed to play sports, drive fast cars, and a myriad of other activities other *normal* teenagers participated in. Andy began to resent the burden placed on his shoulders by his family. Andy became withdrawn, depressed, and somewhat hostile. He accused his family of treating him like a specimen kept in a Plexiglas cage rather than a human being with a mind of his own!

The entire Ashworth family became edgy and agitated with Alex and Alesha because they couldn't seem to control Andy's objectionable behavior. Since Alexa was considered to be the head of his family, it was his responsibility for *handling* his young son! He thought, *The most expedient means of finding assistance was to consult a parapsychologist.* His family had a long history consulting mediums and other unorthodox means of dealing with unmanageable youngsters.

The parapsychologist that they consulted *claimed* to have the ability to delve into Andy's mental sensitivities. She was known for her ability to analyze mystical discernment intuition with foresight into other areas of dealing with the senses.

Mainstream scientists consider parapsychology to be an imitation, quasi-science. Alex fully understood what was involved in the approach that he had chosen for his son. But he was desperate to please his family as well as bring his son under his control. He and his family met regularly to discuss methods of using some sort of *mental infiltration* on young Andy before he became totally unrestrained.

Mental infiltration gives one the capacity to effectively enter into another person's mind and project other thoughts into that person's mind. Someone with such capabilities might be able to persuade their targets to, unknowingly, follow their orders, which is the purpose of mental infiltration. There are numerous maneuvers involved in attempting to enter into the mind of another person.

Methodical penetration of the mind, by any means, has to employ one (or all) of the five major senses. The brain is the *network* through which the senses operate. The brain functions like a computer. It processes whatever information it receives from the senses. Then it sends messages back to the mind, and the body performs whatever the mind relays to it. The mind is the tangible part of human beings that reasons, thinks, feels, motivates, judges, etc. It works as a go-between of the brain and the body.

Seeking the assistance of spiritual intermediaries was common within the Ashworth Dynasty. Following a long discussion with her husband about Andy's behavior, Alesha decided to call in *someone* to assist her in altering the *stressful* behavior of their son.

The Ashworth family knew people whom they believed had *special* intellectual awareness, or psychic abilities. What they didn't know was that the special abilities had been granted at the behest of the devil. At that point, the Ashworths didn't really care.

A medium is termed as one who uses enabling channels through which impressions are transferred to the senses. Mediums intentions are to accomplish a primarily purpose, which is mind control. Alesha convinced herself that the purpose for pursuing *"support"* for Andy was to stabilize his irrational outbursts during the transitional phase of his life. But she really wanted to please the family by permitting her son to come under *their* jurisdiction.

Alesha used trickery to persuade Andy to see the *therapist* that they had selected. Alesha made many empty promises, such as permit him to play sports, buy him a sports car, and participate in other normal things other boys his age did. Alesha also knew that once Andy's mind became subverted by their trusted medium, he would soon lose interest in the things she had promised.

The Ashworth pedigree was more important to Andy's elders than the person himself. To them, Andy represented the hope of perpetuating the family name. Since they were not Christian people, their religious beliefs were worldly. They were wealthy, legendary, and powerful in their own rights. Therefore, anything they needed could be gotten for them at any cost. They did not believe that they were sacrificing Andy for their own self-aggrandizing purposes. The Ashworths convinced themselves that their goal was to seek a higher purpose for Andy.

The devil and his demons were in a triumphant mood after they had succeeded in bringing another Ashworth into their fold. The devil laughingly reminded his demons of a time when he convinced some of God's people to join in the worship of Baal at Peor. Baal has been characterized as a prophet of a Canaanite god. *"Then our ancestors joined in the worship of Baal at Peor"* (see Psalm 16:36). The devil also knew that the worshiping of idols had led to the downfall of the Israelites. *"They worshiped their idols which led to their downfall...and even sacrificed their sons and daughters to demons"* (see Psalm 106:28 and 36–37). Of course, this was a different type of sacrifice, but the principle was the same.

The Ashworth clan were already paying homage to their wealth and status. Unfortunately, the sacrifice of the only heir that could perpetuate their linage was a small price to pay for the future of their family. That is how the devil uses worldly people who love the world and the things in it more than they love anyone else. The Ashworths had placed themselves above everyone else, including God.

Spiritual mediums, fortune-tellers, and other mediators of that caliber are in direct opposition to God's way of dealing with human issues. The Lord proclaimed that those who put their trust in mediums are committing *spiritual prostitution*, and he would turn against them (see Leviticus 20:6).

Mediums represent only one of the methods imposters utilize to gain entrance into the minds of others. Some con artists use *incanta-*

*tions*, which is said to be a magical formula intended to trigger a magical effect on targeted victims. Incantations are allegedly performed by wizards, witches, and fairies during ceremonial rituals and prayers.

There are countless other methods and substances used to invade the minds and spirits of vulnerable subjects. While the devil preys on weaknesses, the Creator doesn't see a believer's weakness as character imperfections. He knows that, in the believer's own strength, he is not able to resist the temptations of the devil. However, the Apostle Paul assures believers that the *Lord will not allow them to be tempted beyond their ability to endure the temptations.* He will even *show them a way out so that you can endure* (see 1 Corinthians 10:13). He will strengthen you and help you if you ask him. The devil knows all this very well. He is counting on believers not to look for ways out. Human beings are born with the same inherent nature that the devil has. Their carnal bodies are accustomed to the pleasure of the flesh. The devil certainly has no love for the well-being of humans, although he attempts to lead people to believe that he cares.

The devil is quite crafty at generating openings for his demons to enter. Once they get inside, they bring in other evil spirits. Believers, who do not attempt to look to the Holy Spirit for a way out of demonically controlled situations, are, in essence, *throwing out a welcome ma*t for mediums and other rebellious spirits to take control of their minds.

The free will of humans is a special gift from God that allows them to make independent choices. God created mankind to love him because they want to, not because they have to. His desire was that people would *choose* to enter into God's will because they want to respond to his love. God had a specific purpose in mind for every human being that he brought forth. But their free will allows them to choose, or reject the destiny that God has planned for them. Each choice will result in like consequences. Rejecting him does not have to be verbally establish. It can occur as a choice of omission, or failure to open the door of one's heart when he hear Jesus, standing there knocking.

The first couple used their free will and *chose* to rebel against God by eating fruit from the forbidden tree. Therefore, they paid the penalty of death or separation from God, which fell on all humanity. *"The wages of sin is death [or spiritual separation from God] but the gift of God is eternal life"* (see Romans 6:23).

The demonically embedded serpent that deceived the first couple in the Garden of Eden is the same devil that was thrown out of heaven because he was seeking enough power to be in control. He is the same devil that goes to and fro through the world looking for someone to consume, demolish, and overwhelm. He knows that he can still persuade mankind to make rebellious decisions because he did it before. He works even harder at his craft since Jesus paid the price for salvation, which reconnects mankind to God through a new birth in Christ! He really wants mankind to use their freedom of choice to rebel against God's will and choose his will instead! He has many weapons in his arsenal and many demons working on his behalf.

The devil constantly attempts to *get into the heads* of people by way of the five senses. Witchcraft is one of the devils most beneficial tools used to alter ones freed will to choose. He uses what some people believe to be innocent burning of incense in a cauldron. A cauldron is a cast-iron pot used to burn loose incense and other substances, which were oftentimes used. However, today, the manipulators use electric diffusers to dispense vapors from heated concoctions to enter their subjects' mind through the sense of smell as well as other senses. Odors, aromas, and fragrances emitting from diffusers are used to infiltrate the mind and weaken the free will of targeted subjects.

Certain *essential* oils, spices, and other combinations of powders and herbs are habitually used in overt close quarters. When targeted subjects enter into specified rooms, the odors permeating the rooms craftily embrace them. The aromas usually have a calming effect, which the brain interprets as a good thing. The brain sends a positive message to the mind. The mind relays the message to the body, and the affected person becomes spellbound, or somewhat hypnotized. Not only does the mind of the affected person come *under the influence* of the manipulator, he also loses control over his free will to make good sound choices. The scents from such admixtures might be passed off as love portions, which are, in essence, another form of black magic.

Jeremiah Johns had dated Charisma Watts for about six months when his friends told him that Charisma was everybody's girl, and she was also a gold digger. Jeremiah had inherited a sizeable sum of money from his grandfather's estate. He owned his own opulent home, drove a fancy car, and was not stingy with favors to those close to him. After hearing the news about Charisma, he had planned on breaking up with her, but she had planned to entrap him and marry him as soon as possible. Upon hearing that Jeremiah wanted to talk to her, Charisma needed some quick assistance from an alternative source to solidify her relationship with him. She made a date to meet at her apartment for their talk. Charisma made a hurried appointment with a consulting mediator from the dark side.

When Jeremiah went to Charisma's apartment to break up with her, he noticed the aroma of a wonderful unidentifiable fragrance the moment he entered into her family room. The scent permeated the room and engulfed him like a warm caress. Jeremiah thought that it was one of those store-bought aerosols that he oftentimes used in his own bathroom. But Charisma had gone to an herbal mixologist, who had mixed a love portion for her. Charisma was told to place the mixture in a diffuser ahead of Jeremiah next visit. So Jeremiah walked right into the trap she had set for him. The moment his nostrils detected the mysterious aroma, the brain was alerted to send a positive message to the mind to command the body to relax and allow the aroma to take control over his being.

Jeremiah had no idea what was happening to him. It was like he was being rocked to sleep, ever so gently! Charisma was sitting very close to him with a heavier sweet odor emitting from her body. She had dressed seductively for the occasion. She looked and smelled extremely appealing to Jeremiah, and he couldn't keep his hands off her! His senses were aroused by the odors, and his body responded in an uncharacteristic manner.

All those sensations occurred almost simultaneously without Jeremiah ever being conscious of what was actually taking place. An example of how rapidly this transpired can be compared to a quick engine check in computerized cars. When a driver turns the key in the ignition, certain lights flash on and off in rapid succession. This engine check occurs swiftly before the engine is booted up. The driver barely notices the quick engine check. That seems to be how quickly the brain receives notification through sensory impulses and sends them back out to the mind, and the mind requires some sort of action from the body.

Subsequently, Jeremiah's will to make principled choices had been altered in the preplanned development. He had involuntarily relinquished his God-ordained will. He had momentarily become *under the influence* of demonic powers. Charisma was only *a willing* channel through, which the devil worked. She was able to be used by demons because her motives were ungodly. Her determination to obtain a share of Jeremiah's inheritance played into the sin of greed and Jeremiah's lack of caution.

Jeremiah's situation was not out of God's hands because he had committed himself to God's will, but this was one of those trials the believers undergo. But he relaxed in *what felt good to the flesh* without looking for a way out. He did not know that he had been duped. Therefore, the devil immediately began to lay a foundation on which he could build a stronghold within Jeremiah's being to keep him under his control. For Charisma to be successful in her plight, she had to continue to follow the advice of the workers of iniquity. Not only was the sense of smell involved in Jeremiah's mental penetration, the sense of sight was also incorporated.

The sense of sight is regulated through the eyes, which generate impulses based on what one visually focuses on. The brain processes the impulses of what the eyes signal to the brain through visual perception. The perceptions sent to the brain, from the senses of smell and sight, had overwhelmingly transformed Jeremiah's will to make right decisions. Seducing spirits were heavily involved in Jeremiah's mental infiltration. Once he came under the devil's influence, by way of demonic-induced seducing spirits, his will was further corrupted through lascivious, erotic behavior that opposed his decent principled values. The devil was not finished with Jeremiah. He knew he had to work quickly before any divine intervention could take place.

He knew how much God loved Jeremiah and had great plans for his life. Therefore, he employed the sense of taste to further solidify his influence over Jeremiah.

The sense of taste allows people to classify substances such as food, which is not to be confused with the sense of flavor. The sense of flavor utilizes both taste and smell sensitivities. The sensory organ of the tongue's taste buds is implemented in the sense of taste to differentiate between sweets, bitters, salty, sour, and appetizing meat flavors. The same stimuli exercised in the senses of sight and smell is repeated. When one sees a delectable well-prepared meal with an enticing aroma, the taste buds are immediately stimulated. Charisma was an excellent cook. Her *consulting* medium told her that a good way to keep Jeremiah *under her control* was to mix small amounts of her bodily fluids into highly seasoned well-cooked foods and feed it to Jeremiah on a regular bases. Charisma's counselor also gave her other methods of maintaining control over Jeremiah. Charisma, who was desperate, adhered to all her counselor's advice.

Jeremiah, who had been meticulous about his appearance, had begun to look disheveled and allow his hair to grow out of control. His parents, Rodger and Millie Johns, became concerned about their son. Whenever they tried to talk to him about his appearance, Jeremiah became overly agitated with them and abruptly ended the conversations. The demonic forces that had taken up residency within Jeremiah's being saw the Holy Spirit of God within Millie and Rodger and caused Jeremiah to rebuff them.

Charisma had moved in with Jeremiah against his better judgment, but he was powerless to stop her. She had even convinced Jeremiah to marry her, but they were only engaged at that time. Mille was acutely aware of the antagonistic effects of what she termed voodoo, which is another name for witchcraft. She told her husband that she believed that Charisma had voodooed their child because his behavior was totally out of character since he had gotten with her! Rodger brushed Millie's observation off by saying that perhaps Jeremiah was just smitten with the girl. But within the confines of his heart, Rodger knew something was wrong. He just didn't know what to do about it.

Millie began to intercede in prayer for her son's deliverance. She knew that her son was under attack and in no position to pray for himself. She decided to plead his case before God in his stead. Knowing that this was an obscure element of the perpetual spiritual war in the earth, she sought divine guidance. Millie was led to Ephesians 6: *"Put on the full armor of God so that you will be able to stand firm against the strategies of the devil."* Millie was aware of the armor, and she began to consciously put on every piece of spiritual armor. Then she began to pray fervently.

After a few days, Charisma was suddenly called away for a family emergency in another state. Millie used that opportunity to visit Jeremiah. She got a wisp of a putrid smell when she opened the door of the pantry to get some crackers for Jeremiah who was having problems with his stomach. Millie searched around in the pantry until she found a closed metal container of solid cooking oil. When she took the lid off, Millie was horrified when she saw what appeared to be an unknown yellowish substance on top of the oil! She immediately showed the container to Jeremiah and asked him, *"What is this?"* However, Jeremiah was in no mental state to process what was happening. Millie began to pray silently. She knew that she had stepped into the devil's domain. She immediately called her prayer partner, Ava, and gave her an account of what she found. She asked Ava to begin interceding for her and her son immediately and meet her at Jeremiah's house right away! Millie had learned early on to seek reinforcement when confronting the devil.

While Millie and Avery were interceding on Jeremiah's behalf, God's grace and mercy kicked in. Jeremiah asked Millie in a little boy's voice, "Momma, what's happening to me? I feel strange." Millie told him that at the moment, she wasn't sure, but she intended to get to the bottom of the mess that he was in. During Charisma's absence, the strength of her portions had become diluted, and the availability of her food laced with evil sources were absent.

When Ava arrived, Jeremiah was amenable to going home with Millie. They wanted to get him in a peaceful place to continue petitioning the Lord on his behalf. Millie wasn't sure of what other evil instruments of bewitchment that she might find in his house. Once they arrived at Millie and Rodger's home, Millie, who was a quasi-barber, offered to trim Jeremiah's hair. When she began to comb his hair, the comb was met with resistance at the base of his skull. Upon further inspection, Millie found what appeared to be long six-stemmed match sticks crossed in Xs that extended from the front of Jeremiah's head down to the nape of his neck. His long hair made the match sticks invisible. Millie got a mirror and showed them to Jeremiah. He yelled, "Take them out!" Millie put on some gloves before taking them out. She took the match stems outside and burned them. They did not burn easily because they seemed to have been coated with some kind of unidentifiable putrid-smelling substance. She dug a hole in the ground and buried the embers and ashes and sprayed the area with a disinfecting solution.

Meanwhile, Ava had called a few more prayer warriors over, and they were in another room interceding. Ava called on the prayer warriors to use the power that Jesus had released to them in Luke 10:19: *"Look, I have given you (power) authority over all of the enemy…and nothing will injure you"* along with other scriptures used to emancipate Jeremiah from the power of the devil and release the power of the Holy Spirit to combat the enemy.

Millie sat Jeremiah down and trimmed his hair. Then she had him take a bath and change his clothes. She took all of Jeremiah's old clothes outside and burned them. While they were praying, Jeremiah became lifeless for a brief moment and fell to the floor. He began to thrash around as if he was in pain! He didn't say anything legible. The thrashing continued for a prolonged period of time and the saints continued to pray. They thought about the demon-possessed man that met Jesus on the shores of Capernaum. The demonic spirits within the man spoke out. When Jesus commanded them to come out of the man, they stubbornly attempted to harm the man before they left his being. *"The demon threw the man to the floor…then it came out without hurting him further"* (see Luke 4:31–35). The prayer warriors believed that a similar act was taking place within Jeremiah. So they continued to pray until Jeremiah relaxed and got up and looked around as if he was seeing all of them for the first time.

They could have sworn that they saw a positive change taking place in Jeremiah's countenance right before their eyes! Jeremiah began to weep as he praised God! He told his mother and the prayer warriors that while he was lying on the floor, he was aware of a dark presence tugging at him, trying to pull him into a dark tunnel. Jeremiah shook his head, saying, "Everything around me was really, really dark. I was being tortured. Then I could hear you all praying. But it sounded like you were far off in a distance somewhere. I tried to use every fiber in my body to just call the name of Jesus. After a long struggle, I was able to say it out loud, '*Help me, Jesus.*' And even that was garbled. The darkness began to disappear and then I saw a glistening white light reaching out to me. I reached back, and I know that it was the Holy Spirit that enabled me grab onto the light and stand up!"

Jeremiah told his mom that he did not want to go back to his house immediately. He wanted to hire someone to go in and pack up all of Charisma's belongings and send them to her. Then he wanted to hire someone to do a thorough sanitizing and cleaning of the house. Before he went back home, he asked the prayer warriors to anoint the house. He had a bewildered look on his face as he asked his mother, "How does one avoid being influenced by demonic spirits?" Millie took a deep breath and asked the Lord for guidance before speaking. She told Jeremiah that there was no one way to avoid the devil and his demons because they were invisibly involved in many of the activities that we participate in.

In this life, righteous people will be confronted with troubles, time and time again, but the Lord will come to their rescue if they ask him (see Psalm 34:19). Millie reminded Jeremiah that she had reminded him on many occasions to trust the Lord with all your heart. Do not depend on your own understanding. Seek *his will in all you do*, and he will show you which path to take (see Proverbs 3:4–6). You know that when something looks too good to be true, it probably is more like a mirage. Millie told Jeremiah that the most important thing for him to understand was who he was dealing with. She took out her Bible and began to read from the Book of Ephesians *6:12–13*. Millie told her son that he should keep his Bible open to that passage of scripture until he knew what every piece of the armor was and what it was used for. She also told him that before he stepped his foot outside the bed each morning, he should dress himself in God's armor. "Your faith was tested," she told her son. "And a faith that cannot be tested is questionable," Millie reminded him.

The old adage *"All that glitters is not gold"* is very true. As far as women are concerned, the Word of God says, *"He who finds a wife finds a treasure and he receives favor from the Lord"* (see Proverbs 18:22). "So, son," Mille continued on, "this woman found you *after your inheritance!* The first thing you should be concerned about in a woman is her spiritual status. It is God who makes a woman a good wife."

Jeremiah's mother asserted that "the enemy used all your senses to invade your mind. One thing I know for sure," she said, "is that you must constantly surrender your entire being to the Lord and *let him transform you into a new person, changing the way you think. Then you will learn to know God's will for you.* His will for you is good, pleasing, and perfect" (see Romans 12:1–2).

Jeremiah smiled as he remembered all the lessons that his parents had tried to instill in him throughout his life. Before, he had taken their words so lightly because they were just *old fogyish* expressions. But now, he was eternally grateful for them. He knew that he would never wanted to travel that route again. So the devil left Jeremiah for a time. But he hung around waiting for another opportunity to presented himself, just as he had left Jesus after he had finished tempting him (see Luke 4:13).

Of course, that demon went on out into the world to look for his next prospect. He knew that an obscure opening through the senses would become available to him soon. And sure enough, he met Virginia (Ginny) Small, a beautiful young woman who had recently given her life to Christ. Ginny had been blessed with a wonderful singing voice. For as long as she could remember, she wanted to be a star. She began singing in the choir at the small church her family attended when she was about six. When she was in her teens, her friends pestered her to make a video and put it on social media because she would never get the exposure she needed at that little church.

Her parents had told her that her time would come when she was ready, and Ginny believed them. Her music teacher convinced her to participate in an annual talent show during her junior year in high school. Someone videoed the show and put Ginny on social media. Within hours, the video went viral. Talent scouts and agents began to pester Ginny's parents about *putting Ginny on the map*. Ginny's parents, Virgil and Jennifer Small, had very little knowledge about the music industry. Therefore, they turned down all the offers of fame and fortune and instead insisted on Ginny completing her education before permitting her to make the decision on her own.

Well, the demons were hovering around Ginny looking for a way to enter into the situation. It didn't take the demons long to infiltrate the mind of Ginny's music teacher, Ms. Sally Gilmore, whom Ginny trusted and adored. Ms. Gilmore wanted to be one of the world's greatest musicians when she was younger. She certainly had been granted enough talent to do so. Before she learned to read, Sally Gilmore was playing the piano. Like Ginny, she played for her church's children's choir as well as various school talent shows. The social media explosion was a long way off; therefore, Sally's exposure was limited. When her musical talents were recognized by one of her teachers in elementary school, the teacher offered to give young Ms. Sally lessons. That wasn't possible because Sally was the oldest of three children. Their mother was a single parent and, oftentimes, worked overtime to make ends meet. It was Sally's responsibility to take care of the two younger children.

Eventually, Sally graduated from high school and went to college on a music scholarship, but the big break that she dreamed of never came through for her. In her estimation, Sally believed that she still had a chance to realize her dream through Ginny. The forces of evil were constantly whispering in Sally Gilmore's ear, "Ginny might be your last chance. You better go for it while you still have a chance." In her desperation, Ms. Gilmore could no longer differentiate the voice of the Lord form that of the devil. She *wanted* to believe that the whispers were coming from God. She knew that God had a plan for her life, but she didn't know that Satan also had a plan for her life.

She knew that faith came by *hearing* and hearing by the *Word of God*. At that moment, she did not hit the pause button for a brief moment to think about what was happening. The demons encouraging her to turn aside from the principled path of reliability offered her an *illusion* of hope. In the interim, she was in the process of being used to destroy Ginny's life using the sense of hearing to do so.

The sense of *hearing* via the ears can play a decisive role in the overall behavior of a person. The auditory nerve controls the ability to hear. It carries electrical waves, or signals to the brain. The brain interprets, or decodes the signals, which establishes sound. Auditory nerve release depends on how the brain interprets, identifies, and characterizes sound stimuli or inducement. Stimulus is a type of energy, which triggers an action or reaction. Therefore, the sense of hearing can be used to generate sounds that can alter one's demeanor. Certain types of music, or certain words have the power to incite emotional positive and/or negative responses. When Satan, the great deceiver, is whispering into one's ear, he incites that person to take on *his* plans for their lives. He can make it seem like one of *their* best ideas.

Ms. Gilmore knew people in the music industry who were always asking her to connect them with new students whom she believed could go far in the industry. Demon spirits were stealing Ms. Gilmore's common sense and replacing it with carnality. The devil was able to set up residency within her mind as well as merged her freedom to make ethical choices with their desires. So before talking to Ginny about the trap that was being set for her, Ms. Gilmore contacted her friend and music producer, Que. She showed him the video of Ginny singing in one of the school's talent shows. Que was impressed and wanted Ginny to do a demo for him with a repertoire of songs. Ms. Gilmore asked Que if they could do this in private because Ginny's parents were naive, and Ginny, being a good kid, did not want to go against their wishes.

Satan had added lying, the trait that he's most famous for, to the deception that Ms. Gilmore had become involved in. She told Que that "if we could do this without pressuring Ginny, I am certain that we could come up with something very good." Que didn't care about anything except making money, so he told Ms. Gilmore to call him when she was ready.

It took only a few weeks for Ms. Gilmore and Ginny to write a few songs and rehearse. Then Ms. Gilmore took Ginny into Que's studio to make the demo on the pretense that she wanted her songs to be copy written and recorded for a later date. Ginny was not aware of what was happening until weeks after the recordings with Que. One night, Ms. Gilmore and Que's management team came to Ginny's home to speak with her parents about signing a contract!

Ginny's parents were surprised and disappointed that Ginny and the trusted Ms. Gilmore had gone behind their back and made elaborate arrangements without their permission. Ginny was just seventeen years old and needed her parent's consent before signing such a contract. Ginny was in shock. She had no idea what was really happening. Mr. Small asked Que's managers and Ms. Gilmore to leave, assuring them that he and his wife would be in contact with them soon. They needed to talk with their daughter alone.

Ginny tearfully explained all that had happened between her and Ms. Gilmore and Que. She told her parents that she didn't even know what a demo was and what one does with it. Ms. Gilmore told her that they were going to Que's studio and show what a recording studio looks like and what occurs when someone makes a record. They told her that they wanted to save her songs so no one else could steal them. Ginny begged her parents to believe her.

Mr. and Mrs. Small were faithful Bible believers. They were in the process of teaching Ginny how to walk by faith. They assured her that they were not angry with her. They were disappointed in Ms. Gilmore, whose hopes of becoming famous had been dashed by situations beyond her control. They told Ginny, "We know that you trusted Ms. Gilmore, and we don't believe she meant to harm you. In her quest to capture something that had been lost to her, she opened herself up to be used by Satan."

Ginny asked, "How does anyone open themselves up to be used by Satan?"

Her father answered. "Satan had loads and loads of demons working on his behalf. He looks for an opportunity to mislead believers who cannot tell the difference between what the demons whisper in their ears from the voice of the Lord. The way you can tell the difference is to ask yourself a few questions before heading off in any direction. The first question is to ask for directions from God about any and everything. The Lord always has good, hopeful, encouraging words of wisdom for you, and the demonic spirits have lies and illusions. The Lord will always tell you the truth, even if you don't want to hear it. You won't hear him in your ear because he is a Spirit, but you will hear in within your spirit. It's like when you know in your heart that something is right, but in your head, you might not be sure of how you know it. Reading the Bible puts you in touch with the Lord. Listening to your teachings about right and wrong is always the right thing to do."

Ginny began to smile. She told her parents that she understood what her dad was saying. Somehow, she felt in her heart that something wasn't right about all that stuff. "They told me not to mention any of it to her parents because they wanted to surprise you! That really didn't sound right," Ginny said. She said she just wanted to please Mrs. Gilmore because she seemed so happy about all that stuff. She promised to pray more and read her Bible so that she would not be tricked again.

Satan had instructed his demon to prey upon the major shortcoming of Sally Gilmore, which was an unfulfilled dream. Sally Gilmore had never asked the Lord what his plan for her life was. She merely believed that if he gave her the enjoyable gift to play music, it was her responsibility to use it to bring glory to herself. The demonic spirit had whispered that sentiment in her ear for as long as she remembered. Sometimes she would hear melodies in her head, and she was able to play those notes to her satisfaction. She was totally oblivious to the fact that God's intention was for her to use those gifts and talents to glorify him! The art of listening might seem ambiguous to the natural mind. Remember, the brain is like a computer. It only decodes the signals it is presented with. What is sent back out to the mind can be *short-circuited* by one's own desires.

A seasoned oncology nurse, who was always present whenever physicians told their patients that they had cancer, especially if the diagnoses were dreadful. At some point during the discussion, the patients just *stopped listening*. Their minds began to wander, and they only heard portions of what was being said. The oncology nurse had to reinforce their diagnoses, sometimes over and over again. Some cancer patients never accepted what was being said to them as true, even though their bodies were showing overt signs of cancer. Seemingly, that was how Sally Gilmore had gone through life, hearing what she wanted to hear, rather than the reality of what was actually occurring. She had attempted to gain fame through a few other students to no avail. But because Ginny's parents succeeded in mediating on her behalf daily, she was protected from the demon's snare.

There are other ways demons use the auditory nerve to influence believers and nonbelievers alike. The energy transmitted by sonic sound waves is an indication of a supernatural current of speed, which is of the nature of sound waves. The pitch and frequency of sonic sound waves can create numerous effects on a person's behavior. Sonic sound waves have been known to be used undetected, yet they have the capability to do irreversible to harm to the brain. Sometimes the high-piercing sound might be compared to a constant intense ringing in the ear of targeted subjects, only much more piercing. In some cases, this type of sound has been used to obtain confessions out of non-guilty subjects for specific crimes.

Using sound as a method to negatively influence someone comes from the author of lies deception and corruption. Randle Conway, a military intelligence officer, was stationed in a foreign nation for a brief period of time. His room had been wired with some sound wave apparatus that was connected to the light switch in the room. Whenever he turned the lights off, Officer Conway would hear what sounded like a swarm of bees permeating his room. Whenever he turned the lights back on, the sounds subsided. Being an intelligence officer, he was immediately alerted that something was amiss. He had the room checked for "bugs," but none were found. The work that Officer Conway was doing would have exposed the underhanded work of many of that nation's leaders. The intention of the leaders was to use sound waves to interfere with Officer Conway's mental capacity. Thus, he would not have been capable of writing up a coherent report if their plan worked out. Officer Conway was a man with unyielding faith in God. As a result of his faith, he trusted in the wisdom, knowledge, and power of God to direct his pathway in his present situation as he had done on numerous other occasions. Because of his special training and expertise in intelligence matters, he was divinely guided to the source of the sound and given the wisdom to dismantle the apparatus undetected. What the devil meant to harm Officer Conway, God turned it around and made it work for his good.

The devil has other techniques that use the auditory nerve to manipulate the mental sensitivity of people. They include but are not limited to subliminal messaging in music and songs. Subliminal messaging is the initial stage of a development that takes place just *below* the threshold (starting point) of conscious awareness. The purpose of subliminal messaging is to affect targeted minds without them being aware of it. Those messages are usually implanted within some type of audio/sound apparatus. Subliminal messages have the ability to discharge powerful suggestions into the subconscious (unaware) mind. This process is used frequently by demons. That's why it is of utmost importance for believers to *"stay alert! Watch out for your great enemy, the devil"* (see 1 Peter 5:8). Be selective in the choices you make in who and what you allow to enter into your space. Television commercials and other propaganda on television have embedded messages aimed at leading believers away from sound doctrines for years.

Sometimes your enemy uses hearing and the sense of *touch* in combination with each other for self-actualization. Touch is an awareness, which is the result of stimulation whenever contact is made with the skin. The message received from the brain responds to a variety of pressures. Someone can *gently stroke* another person along some sensual trigger points, which can automatically produce a sensual response. On the other hand, when a more pressurized contact is made with the skin, a different flight-or-fight response is generated. The skin actually plays a vital role in the overall function of human beings. It has been documented that engagement through skin is a channel by which elements can enter the body. The top layer of the skin is porous, which allows substances rubbed into the skin to enter into one's bloodstream. The effects that ingredients have on the body depend on the substances used and the purpose for using them. The enemy is, unequivocally, aware of all that. He uses the data to fulfill his purposes. Consequently, elements used to infiltrate one's mind can also be blended into lotions, creams, and even perfumes to gain entrance into the human brain.

The five major senses' purposes are to send information to the brain to enable human beings to perceive the world around them. It is of extreme significance to be cautious when trying out new and allegedly different skincare products.

Many demonic strategies associated with witchcraft, black magic, spell casting, seduction, voodoo, and other mind-altering schemes are well-planned. Within the dark province controlled by the *prince* of the material world is a war room where all wicked plans are made. Keep in mind, a prince rules over a specific realm. However, his administrations are subjected to the *king*. The *king* holds the pre-eminent position over the world and all that is within, above, and beyond it. Before the *prince* can put any of his plans into effect, he must seek approval from the *king*. So the king, who is still in control of the material world, is totally aware of all that occurs anywhere at any time by anyone!

On the journey through the labyrinth of the darkness within the material world, some people are seeking clarity regarding the swift transitions taking place in the world today. The steady stream of propaganda and repetitious lies have specific purposes. The prince of this world is using his power to influence the masses. Power-hungry people in high places deliberately indoctrinate multitudes with misleading information. Sound doctrines oftentimes do not sound as appealing to the masses as the vain promises of the enemy of God. Among people in high places are those whose minds have become darkened through demonic infiltration.

It takes divinely allocated spiritual eyes and ears to see and hear the flaws in the propaganda being peddled. The people of God have been warned by the Holy Spirit that "*In the last times, some will turn away from the faith: They will follow deceptive spirits and teachings that come from demons. They are hypocrites and liars and their consciences are dead"* (see 1 Timothy 4:1). So when you observe human beings faithfully following those with *deceptive spirits,* the Holy Spirit will enable you to discern that their moral principles are totally corrupt. Motivated by greed, power, and recognition opens the door for them to become cultic in their behavior.

# Cults and Alternative Religions

There are several classifications, focuses, and idiosyncrasies involving cults and alternative religions. The most important factors are the underlying purpose and creator behind each. Cults have been characterized as socially deviant belief systems, whose administrations are oftentimes hazy. A classic aspect of a cult is the devoutness of its followers, which are directed toward a specific domineering leader. The reverence that cultic members have for their leader is usually disproportionate and misdirected because deception, manipulation, and faulty promises are used to elicit their support. Perhaps the entire premise behind cults is based on money and the power to control.

Because cult supporters *religiously* follow their leader's commands, they are sometimes confused about religion. Although many people associate religion with a deity, which it can apply in some instances, religion is the materialization of faithful idolization of an accepted institution. In essence, one can be religious about anything (i.e., the bag lady *religiously* searches for something discarded in the trash). She does so on a daily basis for the purpose of finding something useful to her.

That is not to say that some cults are not of a religious nature. Some followers are brainwashed into believing that they are worshiping the Lord by way of their particular leader. Many religious leaders have claimed to be prophets sent from *a* god. However, not all alternative religions are cultic and not all cults are religious.

Many religious groups adhere to a set of beliefs pertaining to the origin, characteristics, and rationale behind the creation of the universe. Most of them involve reverential practices and varied celebrations with moral codes of conduct aimed at regulating human affairs. Religions claim to differentiate their practices from those of the world. The world is viewed as a disorganized mass of individuals doing their own thing. Religion is perceived as an organized group of people believing in a God/god, or group of gods.

Alternative religions are usually confined to one or more *limited* options, which prevent the suggestion any other probabilities. The decision as to what options are selected is made by alternative religious leaders. Christianity, which originated from Jesus Christ, is what alternative religions are replacing. The operative word in Christianity is Christ. His followers center their beliefs on teachings from the Bible. The Bible is a collection of divinely God-inspired writings, which reveals a relationship between God and human beings based on agape love. There is so much more to Christianity and biblical teaching than carnal beings have the capacity to retain.

The counteractive solution to the enemy's *backdoor* influence can be found in the Bible. The foundation for cults and alternative religions is laid in the dark and evil province of the devil. He uses religion as a *backdoor* entrance into the minds of unsuspecting victims. Christianity is based on a progressive love relationship between mortal beings and the Lord. The word Christianity means follower of Christ. A believer is someone who has personally confessed with his mouth and believes in his heart that God raised Jesus from the dead. At that point, a believer can decide whether he wants to put in the work, outlined in the Bible, to walk in the footsteps of Jesus. The Holy Spirit will enable him to do that when he surrenders his *will* to the lordship of Christ Jesus. Then he will be transformed, and his mind can be renewed (see Romans 12:1). Many believers decide not to study the Bible, attend church, and follow in the footsteps of Jesus by omission. Those believers have, indeed, been redeemed. They will not spend eternity in hell, but they will miss out on some of the voluminous benefits of revelation knowledge found in the Bible. Some of them wander aimlessly through life and bump into a variety of stumbling blocks.

Hope had been married to Ellis Eberhard for of fifteen years. Without any forewarning, Ellis came home from work one day and announced that he wanted a divorce. At first, Hope thought that he was joking because they had not a disagreement about anything lately. She thought that their lives were going along well. But he convinced her that he was serious. He had been thinking about an *alternative* lifestyle for quite some time but didn't know how to tell her. Ellis assured Hope that no other woman was involved, but he failed to tell her that he was seeing another man. He moved out immediately.

Hope became devastatingly depressed. She attempted to pray and ask God how to handle her situation. She couldn't get her thoughts together as to how she should approach God. She was not as familiar with him as she needed to be. She was not able to differentiate his voice from that of the devil. All the while she was praying, the devil was whispering in her ear, "*Why did God allow Ellis to divorce you? You know, he could have prevented all of that from happening. If he loved you like you think he does, he would have prepared you better for this situation!*" Hope had no idea that it was the devil whispering in her ear. She thought those *whisperings* were totally her own ideas. Consequently, she began to question God, asking, "*Why did you let this terrible thing happen to me?*" Motivated by the devil, Hope directed her anger toward God, all the while becoming more and more depressed. The devil was preparing her for the destiny that he had in mind for her.

Enthrall was one of Hope's closest friends at work. Hope confided in Enthrall about her situation. Enthrall was known as a busy body. So from that moment on, Enthrall took Hope under her wings and began to plan a *new life for her* without Ellis. She assured Hope the first thing she needed to do was get a lawyer to make sure she received everything that she had coming to her, and she just happened to know a good divorce attorney. After learning of Hope's situation, Enthrall began to invite Hope to spend time in her home, where she introduced her to some of her friends. Occasionally, Enthrall would invite a *special group* of friends over, who showered Hope with attention. Unbeknown to Hope, Enthrall and her friends were members of a *special religious* assemblage that offered an *illusionary degree of well-being*. Hope was in dire need of consolation at that time. She was ripe for the plucking.

After learning that, Hope felt totally defenseless, Enthrall told her that she knew of someone who could help her get over her feelings of bleakness. Hope rejected the offer because she thought that Enthrall was referring her to a psychiatrist. But her friend told her magnificent things about her religious counselor instead. Hope was still skeptical because she had tried to contact the pastor of her old church, and he never answered her! Enthrall told her their leader, Dr. Jessup, had led many people to a place where many of their human desires could be met. She went on to say, *"He is very patient and spends personal time with everyone who comes to him and answers whatever questions you might have in simple terms."* Enthrall told Hope that she owed it to herself to at least meet Dr. Jessup.

Hope had no idea that Enthrall was introducing her to a cult leader. Subsequently, Enthrall had no idea that she was a member of a cult. She had become so spiritually blinded until she actually believed that she had found a group of like-minded people, whose leader had their best interest in mind.

A cult is a belief system overseen by an alluring, mystifying leader who covertly commands excessive devotion. The leader uses brainwashing techniques along with conspiratorial speeches to reign in followers. Cultic leaders manipulate their members into opposing wise, balanced reasoning by convincing them that *he alone* can take of their needs. Cultic leaders skillfully disassociate their followers from reality and pressurize to denigrate anyone who dares to leave the fold.

Hope was so distressed until she didn't notice that Enthrall only associated with people who were a part of the group led by Dr. Jessup. But Hope felt that there was something strange about Enthrall's praise and attitude of worship for Dr. Jessup. She couldn't readily identify the problem, but it just didn't feel right to her. As a result, Hope put off meeting with Dr. Jessup until she talked with her mom about her situation.

Hope's mom, Grace, was a single mom who had raised Hope and her younger siblings alone. She was a staunch disciplinarian because she wanted her children to be raised with integrity. Grace insisted on her children going to church and behaving appropriately at all times. Hope thought that her mom was mean. So she couldn't wait to leave home. She had hastily married Ellis without her mother's blessing. Therefore, she had been hesitant to talk with her mother about her present situation.

Hope had accepted Jesus as her Savior, and she had learned many profitable things about him while she lived at home. But she never made him her Lord! When Hope left home, she no longer attended church and began to live life in the *fast lane* with her husband and his friends. When her husband abruptly departed, she felt alone. The evil spirits of darkness were watching her and immediately imbedded Enthrall into her life. Although Hope had not engaged in a real sit-down discussion with her mom in a long time, her mom never stopped interceding in prayer on her daughter's behalf.

Although Hope was not aware of the Lord's presence, his presence was always with her. That feeling that something wasn't right was a nudge from the Holy Spirit. Hope cried out to the Lord, *"Tell me what to do?"* He heard her, and she received a strong urge to call her mom. It seemed like Grace was waiting for her call. They agreed to meet the next day. Hope poured out her heart to her mom before telling her about Enthrall and Dr. Jessup. Grace was aware of Dr. Jessup and his cultic followers. She told Hope many things about Dr. Jessup, cults, and alternative religions.

Grace began by giving Hope a clear picture of what constitutes a cult. "A cult can be defined as a sect, clique, or unconventional assemblage of people who practice extreme worshipful commitment to a charismatic leader. Such groups are usually associated with extremely alternative religious factions that participate in ill-omened exhibitions. There are numerous nonreligious cults as well as religious ones.

"People, from all walks of life, find themselves engaging in cultic lifestyles. All human beings were born with a deep-seated need to give and receive love, a need to feel protected and comforted, as well a desire to communicate with like-minded people. Cultic practices becomes tempting to them because of the deceptive magnetic abilities of the leaders and other members to propagandize a mysterious *impression* of comfort. They bombard newcomers with affection, adoration, and attention. They establish a culture within their sects that positions them [cult members] in a position of resistance against the worldly systems. The leader floats the idea that his members are protected and insulated from the world with him. That idea empowers him to maintain control over his members. He uses brainwashing techniques to persuade members to believe in him.

"Cult leaders usually possess an outstanding ability to manipulate. Their intentions are to utilize an expansive communal influence aimed at generating boundless behavioral changes by infiltrating the minds of followers with their teachings. It has been documented that cult leaders use mind-altering tactics to satisfy their insatiable appetites for the power to control. At some point and time, during the course of their dominating practices, leaders might not be capable of differentiating between reality and truth, or illusions and deception. The real truth is they had an opportunity to receive the love of God that they might be saved. But instead, they found more pleasure in unrighteous activities. Therefore, *God sent them strong delusions that they should be judged and believe lies rather than truth*' [see 2 Thessalonians 2:10–12 KJV].

"Although cultic leaders believe that they are the masterminds behind the cults, in reality, they are merely puppets. Demonic powers of the devil are the real engineers behind cultic practices. The real deceiver, the devil, permits cult leaders to set themselves up as gods. The leaders command worshipful loyalty and devotion to themselves first and their cause second. Even though leaders of cults have skillfully used their demonic power to lead multitudes away from reality, they are not, and never will be, omnipotent (having all power). They can mimic God because they once *knew about* God *intellectually*. Sometimes, knowing about God intellectually versus knowing him spiritually might seem indistinct. However, consciously and intentionally inviting God into one's life enables him to develop a spiritual connection to him. The real question is does God know you that way? There will come a time when God will say to the workers of iniquity, *'I never knew you, depart from me you workers of iniquity'* (see Matthew 7:23 KJV). Acts of deception, immorality, and wickedness are among the most appalling offences used by cultic leaders. Once their members surrender their rights to make independent decisions, the cult leader becomes their god. It's like selling one's soul to the devil and getting nothing of value in return. Seduction is the major tool used to train members' brains to become attached to the cult's beliefs. Once they become mentally and spiritually connected through what they perceive as love and acceptance, they become committed to the leader. Members believe that it was their decision to associate with people who make them feel good at first! The devil fortifies *his* position by building strongholds within the minds and hearts of all who participate in cultic behavior."

While Grace was talking, Hope stopped her to ask, "What's the difference between religion and Christianity?"

Grace explained thusly, "The operative word in Christianity is Christ. Therefore, it is all about Jesus Christ based on the sacred scriptures within the Bible. What it really means to be a Christian is to follow the examples of Jesus and the teachings from the Bible. The behavior of a Christian is opposite of the appalling characteristics of workers of iniquity. Religion can be defined as a central set of principles and practices agreed upon by persons or factions or groups. A cult can be defined as an unorthodox form of religion, by which members sanction the supreme importance of the leader.

"Cult members are led to believe that they are superior to the noncultic population, thus laying a foundation for detachment from family and friends. Once targeted members have become totally inundated, they are convinced to separate themselves from society and buy into whatever the leader is promoting. Most are lulled into giving up their personal possessions." Hope was looking at Grace with a befuddled look on her face.

She asked, "How do you know all of this stuff?"

Grace looked away, and her shoulders slumped a little, as memories of when she was the lowest point in her life rushed to the surface of her mind. She knew that she had to be honest with Hope for her own protection. She got up from the table where they were having coffee and walked over to the window before answering Hope. She began her story thusly, "I thought that I had the perfect life. I thought your father and I were building a forever life together. I ignored all of the red flags when he began coming home later and making excuses about where he was going. I told myself that I trusted him. Although I was not surprised when he told me that our lives together was not working for him, the pain I felt seemed to have touched my very soul! We had been together as friends, long before we got married. The divorce left me feeling empty. I turned away from my faith in God because I felt like God had betrayed me. Unbeknownst to me, my vulnerability made me a perfect recruit for a cult. One of my associates, Valarie, whom I had known for quite a while, invited me come with her to one of her *meditation sessions*. Valarie told me that her meditation guru had helped her get through many critical situations over which she had no control.

"Valarie's meditation guru was a gentle man with a warm smile and soft touch. At his suggestion, we had come a few minutes early so that I could become acclimated to the classes. He asked me if I had ever meditated before under the guidance of a trained specialists. When I answered no, the guru told me that meditation was an uncomplicated way to liberate my mind and create a pathway for me to focus on mental relaxation." At first, Grace said that she didn't know that the guru was a Buddhist priest. She was fervently seeking relief from her emotional upheaval. "So when Valarie promised that getting with her guru and learning to meditate on myself I would eventually find stress-free peace and begin to concentrate on my pathway forward, I jumped at the chanced. She told me that I would begin to sleep better, become emotionally stronger, and have more energy. It seemed like that was everything I was seeking! After weeks of meditation, Grace said that she noticed a transformation taking place in the way she behaved that she could not identify, nor could she control. She merely thought that she was reaching another level of her *conscious self* that she had been told about.

"Her family and even her children, who were small at the time, began to ask her what was wrong with her. She did not want to admit it at first, but her emotional state was getting worse, her social interactions with people outside the meditation group were abnormal, and her sensory perceptions were off-kilter.

"Not knowing what else to do, she said she made an appointment to see her family doctor. When she told him that she could not explain her symptoms, he asked her about any drastic changes that she had made. Grace said that she told him about her meditation classes and the name of the guru teaching the classes. Her doctor's face clouded before he asked her how long had she been attending. When she answered about six months, the doctor recommended a Christian psychologist, who specialized in assisting clients who had, inadvertently, found themselves in the midst of a cult."

Grace said the she felt more lost after deciding to leave the meditation group than she did before she became involved. She was having issues with self-identity, not knowing that she had been mentally battered. The guru talked much about *them* (those who did not meditate properly) and *us* (those meditating under *his* guidance). His gentle inundation was an indoctrination technique. She had become fearful of those the guru termed as them. In essence, what the guru was in the process of doing was attempting to erase her image of her *former self* by telling her that she could only become enlightened if she left all the old stuff an people behind and become energized through an evolution process. It all sounded so good and so positive at the time until she was told that everything was energy, including money. While there was a cost involved in the instructive meditation classes, donations to the cause were strongly advocated. The premise was the more money you gave, the more empowered you became.

Grace was the sole support of her children; therefore, her giving had to be limited to the cost of the classes. As a result, she was sharply rebuked by one of the organization's financial leaders. Grace said that the severe criticism was totally unexpected. Therefore, a bright-red flag found its way to her consciousness. In retrospect, Grace accredited the red flag to the many people, including her mother, who was interceding to God in prayer on her behalf.

Grace's trust had been shattered, and she was uncertain about meeting new people. But she told her daughter that she decided to make an appointment with the psychologist, Ms. Bailor, whom she had been referred to. Ms. Bailor knew that Grace, like a number of other clients she had seen, was skeptical about someone else entering into the restricted areas of her mind. So she began her session by telling Grace all the things that she believed she was experiencing. Grace said she relaxed a bit after the introductory remarks.

"Ms. Bailor assured me that meditation within itself was not a bad thing. As a matter of fact, the Lord told Joshua to '*study the Book of instructions continually. Meditate upon it day and night so that you will be sure to obey everything written it. Only then will you prosper and succeed in all you do*' (Joshua 1:8). *What* you are meditating on makes all the difference in the world. The meditation guru that you were sitting under was a Buddhist. He encourages his pupils to believe as he does: The pathway to clarity, strength, and power (enlightenment) is attained through the practice and development of virtue by way of meditation and wisdom. That chant that they encourage their pupils to do to prepare themselves for meditation is a shrouded way of changing one's personal commitment. The chant is somewhat of a declaration of loyalty and devotion to the mystic law of Lotus Sutra, which they believe is the good law of truth."

Grace said that Ms. Bailor explained to her that she was unintentionally engaging in an alternative religion that contradicted Christian principles. Grace did remember the instructor talking about becoming enlightened a lot. She said that she assumed that enlightenment meant become more aware of things in her world. The psychologist informed me that enlightenment meant something different for Buddhist than it did within the Christian community. In some of the alternative religions, including Buddhist, it means an absolute higher form of awareness characterized by belief in the power of *human* reason, among other things. Biblically, enlightenment is often interchangeable with *divine* illumination, revelation, salvation, and conversion. The Apostle Paul's prayer for the Ephesians was "*I pray constantly for the Lord to give you spiritual wisdom and insight so that you might grow in your knowledge of God*" (see Ephesians 1:17). In other words, he was praying for them to become illuminated or enlightened as the Spirit reveals such thing as they *needed* to know to share in the power of God! Grace said that she was surprised to learn that what she believed to be innocent self-help routines was really cultic practices. She laughed as she told Hope, "I was truly *enlightened* when I left Ms. Bailor's office."

Grace told Hope that she had a few more sessions with Ms. Bailor before she felt whole again. On her last session, Ms. Bailor gave her a sheet of paper with some scriptures written on it, which she called rescue and deliverance. "She encouraged me to return to the Christian community for spiritual growth." Grace pulled out the sheet and shared this with Hope from Ephesians 3:14–19: "*I pray that from His glorious, unlimited resources He will empower you with inner strength through His Spirit. Then Christ will make His home in your hearts as you trust Him. Your roots will grow down into God's love and keep you strong and you will have the power to understand, as all God's people should, how wide, how long, how high, and how deep His love is. May you experience the love of Christ, though it is too great to understand completely. Then you will be made complete with all the fullness of life and power that comes from God.*"

Hope asked another question before departing, "Do you think that all the pandemonium and chaos within the political area has something to do with demonic forces within the earth?" Grace said that they did not have to speculate anymore. All they had to do was look to the prophecies of old within the Bible, and the answers were all there.

Grace said, "I don't claim to know about the times when some of the things spoken of in the Bible will come to fruition. However, when I compare the prophecies of old with the reality of what is actually occurring, I believe that each day brings us closer to the end times. There are numerous scriptures that reveal what will occur during the end of time as we know it. That's why during these times, Christians need to be able to recognize the difference between heaven-bound citizens (Christians) and hell-bound citizens (worldly people). It seems like there is a race among people to see who will be in charge of someone else. The unquenchable aspirations for the power to control is dangerous. It's like people's lives and livelihood are on an action block and being sold to the highest bidder."

Grace took out her Bible and turned to 2 Timothy, third chapter, and began to read verses three through five to Hope, "*But understand this; that in the last days there will come times of difficulty. For people will be lovers of self, lovers of money, proud, arrogant, abusive, dis-*

*obedient to parents ungrateful, unholy, heartless, unappeasable, slanderous and without self-control, brutal, not loving good, treacherous, lovers of pleasure rather than lovers of God, having the appearance of godliness but denying its power... Avoid such people."*

Hope seemed mesmerized after Grace stopped reading! In a whisper, she said, "Momma, as you were reading, I saw the faces of many of this nation's leaders appear before my face. Are you saying that that is why we are undergoing such swift and destructive transitions in this world?" Grace assured her daughter that *she* was not saying anything. She was merely reading prophecies from the Bible. Hope asked, "What are we to do?" Grace turned to the Book of Luke and read, *"But stay awake* [alert] *at all times, praying that you may have strength to escape all the things that are going to take place, and to stand before the Son of Man"* (21:36). Grace took Hope back to verse eleven to give her a brief overview of what to expect in the last of days. *"There will be great earthquakes, and in various places famines* [deprivations, deficits, poverties lack of food] *and pestilences* [widespread viruses and diseases] *and there will be terrors and great signs from heaven."* Hope squealed out, "Oh my god, Momma, many of these things are happening right now!" Grace assured Hope that according to the Scriptures, "no one knows the day or the hour that the day that Christ will return, not even the angels of heaven nor the Son of God, but the Father only" (see Matthew 24:36).

Grace and Hope embraced, with the assurance the deliverance was always available through Christ! They both understood that cults and other mind-infiltrating tactics were weapons that the devil and his demons used to attack the people of God. They also understood that the same tactics were used to keep those under their influence from straying from the fold. However, they both learned that the battle within the spiritual world had spilled out into the material world. But the battle was not theirs to fight. It belonged to the Lord. As long as they remained faithful to the Lord, they would be safe.

# Deliver Us from the Evil One

Thus far, we have traveled up and down many highways and byways and beheld the lives of a number of characters. We caught glimpses of some of the evil means, methods, and manipulates of the devil and subsequent dilemmas arising from each. But we've only touched the tip of the iceberg regarding tactics, tricks, and mental-modification vehicles used by devil. His mission is to gain the power to control his victims. Now that *we know what we know,* the time has come for each believer to ask for *divine* guidance as we venture on to taking the next step forward.

Deliverance has multiple meanings, but the primary focus here will be placed on *being set free* from the power of the devil. Deliverance also embodies being released from captivity after being held hostage by the devil. The basic discussion here will highlight cleansing from the effects of demon spirits. All born-again believers have already been delivered from the *consequences* of sin. The penalties of sin includes death (separation from God) and eternity in hell. "Jesus said, '*I tell you the truth, unless you are born again, you cannot see the kingdom of God*'" (see John 3:3).

While salvation saves believers from spending an eternity in hell, it does not prevent believers from sinning. Redemption enables believers to resist the temptations from the devil. Sometimes unresolved issues can prevent believers from using their power to resist the devil. Spiritual deliverance addresses the core issues, *under the guidance of the Holy Spirit.* Successful spiritual deliverance is *always* an act of God. But throughout life, believers will be tempted by things that the flesh remembers well. A mind that is not continuously renewed will relay carnal ideas to the body, which will cause the believer to sin. There will even be times in the lives of believers when they seek deliverance from sources other than the Lord.

Mystic Cringe had a shingle hanging in front of her modest home that read, "*Spiritual healing.*" Mystic claimed to have the "*divine gift*" of healing, which was inundated with demonic spirits. She widely broadcasted the claim that she was able to deliver people from the clutches of the black magic spells. Throughout any given day and into the night, people streamed in and out of Mystic's house. Her house had a heavy smell of a unknown substance. Her *healing station* was a dimly lit room with a comfortable couch, a few chairs, and a table with an open Bible on it. There was also a group of shelves with a display of aromatic oils and other portions that she sold to her clients.

Mystic was always dressed in a long immaculate white robe-like garment. A diamond cross on a gold necklace dangled from her neck. Her nails were perfectly manicured, and she wore a white turban on her head. She offered her clients a seat at the table across from her and began each "*deliverance*" session by reading from Psalms: "*Many are the afflictions of the righteous: but the Lord delivers him out of them all*" (see Psalm 34:19). Then she would listen intently to her client's issues before taking anointing oil from her shelf and dabbing some on her client's forehead and beginning to pray in her what she termed her heavenly language (unknown tongues). She would demand all the demonic spirits to leave her client (calling the client by name). She would read from the book of Psalms again: "*Then they cried out to the Lord in their trouble and He delivered them out of their distress*" (see Psalm 107:6). Mystic would then lay her hands on her client's forehead and command them to cry out to the Lord in a loud voice, which ended the session.

Mystic told her clients that the true manifestation of their healing might not come immediately. Meanwhile, she sold them portions to drink and oils to rub on their bodies. She also encouraged them to come back for love portions, money portions, and other *treatments* at a discounted fee.

Whether her clients were delivered from evil spirits or not was never verified. But her business seemed to have been lucrative.

Mental, spiritual, and even physical invasion by demonic spirits play pivotal roles in spiritual warfare between good and evil. In view of who and what is involved in the enhancement of evil spirits, the goal of deliverance should be to seek an entity more powerful than the devil. Know *what spirit* has empowered the *alleged* healer before seeking deliverance from her. There are many Christ-centered principles believers should engage in before seeking divine deliverance from unorthodox sources, like prayer.

To begin with *know* without a doubt who and whose you are. Then search the Scriptures for answers. If you are of Christ, *"you belong to God, my dear children… He who lives in you is greater than the spirit that lives in the world"* (see 1 John 4:4). He says explicitly, "Do not believe everyone who *claims* to speak by the Spirit. You must test them to see if the Spirit they have comes from God. *There are many false prophets in the world. If a person claiming to be a godly prophet acknowledges that Jesus Christ came in a real body, that person is of God. But if someone does not acknowledge the truth about Jesus, that person in not from God"* (see 1 John 4:1–3).

It's not just words that make the difference here. But some believers don't readily acknowledge the power of the Spirit of Christ that dwells within them. A true prophet or messenger that speaks from God and is being carried along by the indwelling Holy Spirit. False prophets are under the influence of spirits that are detached from God. Therefore, true confessions do not come from an intellectual place but, rather, from a spiritual place. The Holy Spirit demonstrates his presence and power in the lives of believers by enabling them to believe. It is the reality of God in the life of the believer that motivates him to acknowledge genuine truth.

Nonbelievers, seeking deliverance from unorthodox healers or messengers, the best possible advice is go to Romans 10:9–10, which says, *"Confess with your mouth that Jesus is Lord and believe in your heart that God raised him from the dead, you will be saved."* Once anyone, intentionally, invite Jesus Christ to come into their lives, the Holy Spirit will make his home within them. And divine deliverance will be available to each of them.

Once a nonbeliever becomes a believer, God bestows very precious spiritual gifts on them in accordance with his will and purpose. A spiritual gift is a very special, divine, empowering, and prospering ability bestowed on every believer by the Holy Spirit. Each gift is given so that each believer can be equipped to minister as God has predetermined. Every gift is an expression of God's grace and is to be used to benefit the body of Christ and bring glory to God.

*"There are different kinds of spiritual gifts but the same spirit is the source of them all, just as there are different kinds of service, but we all serve the same God"* (see 1 Corinthians 12:4). Each gift is imparted to fulfill a God-ordained purpose. The gift of healing is one of many. It is a divine means whereby the grace of God uses the recipient of the gift as an instrument through, which he makes people mentally, spiritually, emotionally, and physically whole (see 1 Corinthians 12:9 and 28–30). There's the gift of *administration,* by which God enables the recipient to guide the body toward the attainment of God-given goals and dictates. *Apostles.* Divinely empowered to carry the gospel to new perimeters and offer leadership over church bodies as well as maintain control over spiritual matters pertaining to the church. *Discernment.* Whereby receivers are empowered to distinctly differentiate between truth and inaccuracy by assessing whether behavior and teachings within the body, are from God, from the devil, or human mistake, or decision to gain power. *Evangelism.* Beneficiaries of this gift become messengers of the gospel and fulfill the mandate to go, teach, baptize, and such things commanded by the Lord in Matthew 28:19–20. *Prophecy.* By giving the word of prophecy, God uses his appointees to speak as his messengers to his people. The gift of *pastoring* is an extremely significant gift. A pastor is responsible for spiritually guiding, caring for, protecting, and feeding a group of believers entrusted into his care by God. A pastor is accountable to God (see Ephesians 4:11). There are numerous other gifts indicated throughout the Bible. Those gifts fit into the comprehensive plan God has for his people as a unified body of believers. But there is an inordinate number of believers whose gifts *seem to be hidden* because they have deviated from the path God charted for them.

When believers fail to use the gift that the Holy Spirit endowed them with and instead *choose for themselves* another gift, they are, in essence, saying to the Spirit, "I no longer recognize you as the potter who has made me after your will. Therefore, I will get out of my lane and drive in the lane of my choice!" Such believers, often time, collide with other believers who are functioning in their lane.

When two opposing thoughts, ideas, bodies, or other animated objects attempt to occupy the same space at the same time, a collision usually occurs. Collisions are generally demonstrated by strong confrontational disagreements between the parties involved. When believers choose get out of their lane, God views their ill-selected decisions as sinful acts of rebellion.

Not only have their unacceptable thoughts defied the laws of nature that no two objects can occupy the same space at the time, they have cause the believer to disobey God! Like consequences always follow acts of deliberate disobedience. Whatever you give out, it shall be dispensed back to you in the same quantity that you rendered it. Obedience is rewarded, and disobedience is chastised.

God also provides his children with talents, not to be confused with spiritual gifts. Talents are associated with human skills and passions. Some people have, what is termed, n*atural abilities,* such as drawing, singing, and playing musical instruments without being taught professionally along with numerous other abilities. Oftentimes, people use their talents as means of earning financial support. There are other talents or skill sets represented by instinctive passions, such as cooking, sewing, decorating, and the likes. All the things that people are naturally skilled at can be combined with their spiritual gifts, or can be used separately, to bring glory to God.

In this demonically controlled domain known as the material world, the prince of this domain puts forth his best effort to convince believers to use their gifts and talents on his behalf. He promises them lucrative compensations, which he can and does, occasionally, deliver on. He even convinces people to use the gift of healing to *pretend* to cast out demons. However, if the *alleged healer* is not casting out demons under the authority of the name of Jesus, their performances are ineffective. When attempting to cast out demons, or demolish strongholds, it is of utmost important to be led by the Holy Spirit. It is the power of God that the demons recognize and flee.

While Jesus was ministering on Earth, a demon-possessed man who was blind and couldn't speak was brought to him to be healed. Jesus healed the man, his eyes were opened, and his tongue was loosed. There was group from a particular *"religious"* sect in the crowd who accused Jesus of being empowered by the prince of the material world to cast out demons. Jesus, who knew their thoughts informed them that *"If Satan is casting out Satan he is divided and fighting against himself. His own kingdom will not survive…"* (That is not likely to happen.) He went on to say, *"But I am casting out demons by the Spirit of God… Tell me, who is powerful enough to enter the house of a strong man like Satan's house* [domain of Satan] *and plunder his goods* [demolish strongholds]? *Only someone who is stronger"* (see Matthew 12:22-29). Human beings are neither stronger nor more powerful than Satan. But believers, indwelt with the Holy Spirit, are empowered by the Spirit to render Satan and his demons defenseless.

In Jesus's day, his disciples were amazed that when they used Jesus's name, the demons obeyed them! Jesus told them that he saw Satan fall from heaven like a streak of lightning. When he sent them out, he had also empowered them to take authority over all the power of the enemy so that nothing could harm them, not even Satan himself (see Matthew 12:17–18). The same Spirit of God, who raised Jesus from the dead, lives within every believer (see Romans 8:10–11).

Thus far, you have been made aware of various devious tactics used by the enemy to gain entrance into the mind of believers. His major goal is to turn their minds away from things leading toward eternity with the Lord, toward the profane things of the world. He knows that *"as a man thinks in his heart so is he"* (see Proverbs 23:7 KJV). Therefore, he works diligently to put evil thoughts into the minds of believers. He uses reading materials and television programs, especially commercials regarding greed and gluttony, to gain control of believer's minds. Entrenched thoughts are not responsible for the actions that follow, unless the believer allows them to hang around. Once the believer begins to mull over diversionary thoughts, the enemy begins to craftily devise schemes to bring his plans to pass.

Case in point. Someone perceived as very wealthy takes out an ad on a popular television station. He shrouds his idea within an attractive advertisement of a *"simple"* get-rich-quick scheme. Assuring his audience that *all they have to do* is sign up for a seminar *with their credit card.* He throws in "Hurry. Seating is limited. Only a small fee to defray the cost of the seminar will be deducted from your credit card." The enemy whispers in the ear of a believer obsessed with greed, "Here's your chance!" The advertisement shows numerous *allegedly prosperous* people with testimonies regarding how much wealth they amassed through this program. The believer begins to fanaticize about living his dream. With some nudging from the enemy, he signs up for the seminar and finds himself paying a larger sum of money than expected for the package! The enemy found the smallest opening and, quickly and covertly, slid right into the believer's mind.

*Before* believers become obsessed with unethical thoughts and ideas, he should do the following. Push the pause button and think about the pros and cons. Acknowledge God by asking, "Is this a means of swindling me?" Use the power of the indwelling Holy Spirit to demolish urgings and every other pretension that sets itself up against the wisdom of God's point of views (see 2 Corinthians 10:5). Once the believer *quickly* cast any unethical thoughts from his mind, the center of his being he is prepared to become fully obedient to the lordship of Christ. Even after a believer has been led away from righteousness and found himself in the midst of ungodliness, he needs to know that God has not abandoned him. God really wants to cleanse believers of the influences that evil, demonic spirits are choreographing within their minds. The Lord says, *"Come now, let's settle this. Though your sins are like scarlet. I'll make them as white as snow"* (see Isaiah 1:18).

There is indeed a spiritual warfare going on in the invisible realm of the earth. That war is very real. The influences of that war are occurring in the real world. The focus of the perpetual battle is power and control. In view of that, believers must be very clear regarding the fact that human entities *cannot* use human intellect to outsmart the devil, nor can they employ human strength to win the battle against him. The devil knows so much more about so many things than humankind gives him credit for. Followers of Christ should believe with all that is in them that the hostile conflict, that they are significant players in, is not against mere flesh-and-blood entities, although the conspiratorial efforts of the devil will lead unsuspecting believers to *think* that their sisters and brothers are their real enemies. But instead of lashing out at other believers, look to the Word of God for guidance. It will assure believers that the real enemies are the evil rulers of the mighty powers in the dark world as well as evil spirits in heavenly places (see Ephesians 6:12). Therefore, the weapons that the saints of God *should* be using are weapons prepared by God, which are the belt of *truth* and the body armor of God's *righteousness*. God's truth is quite different from the simple definition as opposite of deception. Truth, in this instance, means an inner freedom that flows from God. It is descriptive of the mind, force, resolve, and actual nature as well as the glory of God. Righteousness indicates that the saint should clothe himself in the same incorruptibility, purity, and appropriateness that identifies him with God. He puts on the peace that comes from God for shoes because saints have to stand firm against the devil and his demons. To stand firm against such a challenging foe, the saint must be free from all inner conflicts and instabilities.

Godly peace ushers in a harmonious Spirit and with it comes completeness and wholeness in Christ. Once the saint is free, principled, and peaceful, he holds up the shield of faith to stop the fiery arrows from penetrating the amour, put on the helmet of salvation to protect the renewed mind, and take the sword of the Spirit, which is the Word of God. The saint will be fully dressed to be strong in the mighty power of God (see Ephesians 6:10–13).

Human beings will continue to attempt to use worldly weapons to fight spiritual wars until they are certain of who they are and who the real enemy is. This type of uncertainty *enables the* enemy take control of one's thought process. Whenever believers begin to promote their self-importance, you might guess that the enemy is influencing their thoughts. Can you imagine how hard the devil must be laughing when he has provoked someone to spew out their anger on another human entity? Until believers have firmly established his righteousness through Christ, the devil will continue to use them.

Here is what the enemy is preventing believers from doing once he gains entry into their minds: He prevents them from understanding that, as believers, they are not *humanly* equipped to wage war with spiritual enemies. He doesn't want them to know that they have God's mighty weapons at their disposal. It is of paramount importance to understand what deliverance is.

Deliverance is the emptying, or decontamination process, which rids people of demonic spirits that have penetrated their minds and altered their principled behavioral patterns. Before Christ came in the flesh, walked among men, and returned to glory to be with the Father, all humankind were prisoners to sin. By his death on the cross, as an offering for the sins of humankind, Christ paid humanity's get out of jail bail. He made deliverance from the consequences of sin available to everyone willing to accept his priceless offer.

The enemy uses his authority keep people under his influence, submissive to him by burdening them with anxieties, suspicion, and other ungodly traits. Most of his victims do *not believe* that they have issues that need to be addressed. They have become spiritually blind to the truth. They can be delivered from the evil forces that possess them. In reality, all the devil's victims are mentally, emotionally, and sometimes, spiritually imprisoned. Only an unrestrained entity more powerful than the devil can rescue or deliver them. God uses committed saints as empowered instruments to set them free.

Imagine a person being picked up by the police and placed under arrest on any given day. The arresting officers disarm prisoners by taking all their personal possessions. They tell the prisoner that he can be released, but he must put up a monetary bond to assure the officers that he will return for his court hearing. He is given the opportunity to make a phone call. He calls someone who is *not in bondage* to pay his bail. Although he might have plenty money in his wallet, his wallet is not available to him. People in bondage to the enemy are in a similar situation, but demonic incarceration is much more dangerous. The enemy of God (and man) is competing for the very soul of his victims.

You might ask, "How can one readily identify the enemy?" According to the Word of God, *"you can tell a tree by the fruit it bears"* (see Luke 6:43). That verse speaks of one's *demonstrated* character traits as identification. Watch what they do versus hearing what they say. The enemy practices hostility against believers in whom he sees Holy Spirit living within. He actively opposes followers of Christ by attempting to weaken their will to make principled choices. Their behavioral alterations manifest themselves emotionally. His victim exhibits anger, jealousy, rivalry, and envy as well as other antagonistic traits against believers. Satan and his deceitful workers even try to disguise themselves as angels of light to trick people into believing they are righteous messengers. *"Even Satan disguises himself as an angel of light. No wonder that his workers disguise themselves as servants of righteousness"* (see 2 Corinthians 11:14).

Satan needs a body to accomplish his reprehensible deeds. Therefore, when believers encounter his unprincipled demons functioning within the minds of human beings, believers should fervently pray for guidance before attempting to rescue them. Jesus has left a road map for saints to follow. Galatians 6:1 says, *"Dear brothers and sisters, if another believer is overcome by some sin, you who are godly should gently and humbly help that person back onto the right path. And be careful not to fall into the same temptation yourself."* Just how you do that? First, you pray for the Holy Spirit to guide you when go to the brother or sister with godly love in your heart. Have a one-on-one conversation. Then do as the Apostle Paul did. *Greet them with words of encouragement versus accusatory dressing down.* Be willing to share the sister or brother's burden so that you are obeying the law of Christ (see Galatians 6:2–3). Everything must be done in humility and to the glory of God. Your spiritual ears must be open so that you can hear his voice; otherwise, you will speak from an intellectual place. That will render your efforts ineffective. Grace and mercy *will not* come without humility. There must be a spirit of genuine forgiveness within the heart of the messenger of God. Divine deliverance *cannot* occur without the anointing.

Anointing means to be set apart, empowered, and protected for the purpose of accomplishing God's work. It is God who has empowered and enabled (anointed) the saints to stand firm in Christ. He commissioned them and identified them as his own by placing the Holy Spirit in their hearts (see 2 Corinthians 1:21). He protects them by his command: "*Do not touch my chosen people and do not hurt my prophets*" (see 2 Chronicles 16:22). Messengers of God must see themselves as instruments when they are in his will and doing *his* work. They should never allow themselves to become puffed up.

No human being is powerful enough to liberate another person from the clutches of Satan. That is why it is of paramount importance that you function under the power of the Holy Spirit and leave the results up to God!

Without the power of the Holy Spirit, the door opens for Satan to walk right in and harm them. Today, the evil spirits operating within sisters and brothers recognizes the Holy Spirit that dwells within the saint. But if a believer has used his *free moral agency* (will to decide) to function from his own *rational* viewpoint versus the wisdom of God, he is outside the will of God. God perceives his poor choice as sin. God *does not* look *favorably* upon sin from anyone at any time (see Habakkuk 1:13). Believers should always seek God's favor in everything. "*Why are you worrying about the speck in your friend's eye when you have a log in your own*" (see Matthew 7:3)? Seeking God's approval is an example of trusting his perfect will over your imperfect will. God looks upon repentance and forgiveness favorably.

Saints are to approach each other with the attitude in which Christ would approach them. Here's what the Word says about that: "Show encouragement because you belong to Christ. Comfort in love, Fellowship in the Spirit with tender hearts and compassion. Don't be selfish or try to impress others. Be humble thinking of others better than yourselves" (see Philippians 2:3). Jesus gave up his divine privileges in glory and took on the position of a slave for the salvation of all who would believe! What a privilege it is to become a servant!

If the Spirit is not in control within one's heart, even unforgiven and unforgiving believers can fall prey to the enemy's tactics. Therefore, it is never okay to attempt to rescue another person unless you were commissioned by God to do so. Without the power of divine anointing, no one can command evil spirits without suffering adverse consequences. The evil spirits recognized and addressed Jesus as the holy one sent from God. How will the evil spirits address you?

Not everyone *obsessed* with evil spirits wants deliverance. There is an excessive number of people, with whom saints interact on a regular basis, who oppose God as the supreme authority. Existing within the material world in which the saints of God live is the actual Church of Satan. That is a *religious* organization that views Satan as the irrefutable epitome of enlightenment. To the congregants, Satan represents pride, individualism, knowledge, insight, and cleverness. Their devotion to their doctrinal principles supports their consummate contempt for the Christian faith. They study from a Satanic Bible, which is a compilation of compositions, dissertations, rituals, and articles published by the church's founder in 1969. To the founder and membership, their Bible is characterized as their most important document. The leaders use it to influence modern-day Satanism. The Bible of Satan challenges the Ten Commandments and the golden rule. Their leader promotes a doctrine that is centered on seeking pleasure and self-gratification in a modest way. They believe that pleasure, sensuality, and carnality will bring about the greatest good in a person and usher in a state of tranquility. Concepts from the Book of Lucifer comprises most of the twelve chapters in the Satanic Bible. Major topics of discussions within those twelve chapters include their perceptions of indulgence/leniency, love, hate, and sex.

It is believed that the Church of Satan is an offspring of Luciferianism. But each has an entirely different belief systems. Most people characterizes Lucifer as the shining one, or light bearer. The expressions bringer of the dawn and morning star has also been associated with Lucifer when he resided in heaven. However, the proper name for Lucifer is said to be "Devil."

There is much written about Luciferianism, which is a mixture of philosophy and other unfounded historical accounts. Isaiah addressing Lucifer, "All your pomp has been brought down to the grave... *How have you fallen from heaven o shining star, you who destroyed the nations of the world...*" (see Isaiah 14:11–12)?

It has been said that Lucifer's self-importance played a pivotal role in his downfall. Luciferianism is a belief system whose followers reverence and worship the fundamental qualities of Lucifer. Supporters of the Luciferianism sect esteem, idolize, praise, and worship Lucifer as an emancipator, protector, and guiding spirit. Lucifer is perceived as the true god who opposes the Almighty God. Lucifer, Satan, the devil, and numerous other interchangeable names describe him. He has numerous traits that his worshipers have adopted, such as liar, accuser of the saints before God, deceiver, highly sexual (even bisexual) oppressor, murderer, and tempter to name a few. If you might be wondering, what does all this have to do with you? Well, within the material world, which is now the devil's domain, people with whom your paths cross with are from all sorts of religious sects. They are forever recruiting new followers using different *higher-ups* and touting similar propaganda.

The nature of Lucifer/Satan's rebellion against God was pride and self-will, just as the nature of those who willfully chose to rebel against God's perfect will for their lives today. Even some saints, whom God has blessed with divine wisdom and knowledge, as well as other gifts and talents from his treasure trove, are still becoming filled with pride and narrow-mindedness from the same ancient source. But Jesus Christ offers them repentance and forgiveness and the privilege and opportunity for God's favor to shine upon them.

Today, followers of the leadership of the Church of Satan and worshipers of Lucifer were all created as free moral agents with the *capabilities* to make their own choices. They are like people spoken of earlier on in this narrative who knew the truth about God because he made it obvious to them. But they shamelessly refused to worship him as God, or even give him thanks. They began to contemplate preposterous ideas of what God was like. As a result, their minds became darkened and confused. They have already been abandoned by God to do whatever shameful things they desire (see Romans 1:20–21, 24). People intentionally exhibiting the traits of Lucifer/Satan should be recognized as the enemy of God. Saints should carefully determine what pleases God and refuse to participate in any other evil and dark deeds. Make the most of these evil days. Seek

Spirit-guided relationships but accept each other out of reverence to the Lord Jesus Christ (see Ephesians 5:10, 16, and 21).

In today's society, we witness profane, sacrilegious leaders in high places revealing to the world who they are by their deeds and language. Believe them when they prove to you who they are! The magnitude of immoral, corrupt people seems to be rapidly growing. But saints were told about these things beforehand. Therefore, when the earthquakes begin to occur in unusual places and famines and plagues reach worldwide pandemic phases, saints should remember that they were told these things would happen. The simplicity of golden rule—do to others whatever you would like for them to do to you—can keep believers in perfect peace because they will be in the will of God. This is the essence of all that is taught in the law and the prophets. You can *only* enter God's kingdom through the narrow gate. That is the hope of every human being. But the work must be done before anyone can enter through that gate. The highway to hell is broad, and its gate is wide, for *many* will choose that way. "But the gateway to life [eternal with Christ] is very narrow and the road is difficult, and only a few will find it" (see Matthew 7:12–14). Gate is a metaphor, or symbolic representation of Christ Jesus. Jesus told his disciples (for all times), "*I am the way the truth and the life. No one comes to the Father except through me*" (see John 14:6). He is the gate through, which one must pass through to reach eternal life. In this instance, narrow is referring to a select distinct group of transformed individuals who have undergone and overcame sin. The ones who enter in through the narrow gate have made and kept commitments, repented for their sins, and focused on holy living. Few will find the narrow gate because they made *decisions* to take the path of least resistance and follow the crowd. They would not be able to find the narrow gate because they were going in the wrong direction!

Imagine, if you will, a freeway-like road with about ten smooth paved lanes. That road is very long, broad, and wide with merchants of diver's sorts all along the way. Each merchant's wares are enchanting and enticing. Their stands are brightly arrayed to attract attention. The wares on sale appeals to as many human desires as possible. There are even beautiful scantily dressed females with bodies *to die for on that road.* There are shirtless muscular men displaying their physiques. Mortals traveling along this road are totally unaware of the evil spirits whispering to their carnal minds. The invisible evil spirits are influencing them to partake of the goods available to them. They don't know that this road leads to hell, and the longer they stay on that road, the closer they get to the destination they chose!

Of course, it goes without saying very few people *overtly choose* to spend eternity in hell. Nevertheless, the same choice has been set before each individual. The call to return to the Lord began in the Book of Deuteronomy. *"Now listen! Today I am giving you a choice between life* [eternal] *or death* [in hell], *between prosperity and disaster. For I command of you to this day to love the Lord your God and keep His commands,"* says the Lord (see Deuteronomy 30:15). Rebelliousness against the Lord's commands buys a one-way ticket to hell.

The gate leading to eternal life with the Lord is probably very narrow, somewhat rugged, and unpaved with no glaring lights and shining objects along the way. Jesus himself illuminates the way. There are no merchants at all because the road is too narrow. The elect of God will be traveling up that road. The elect *chose* to show their love for God by obeying his commands (see 1 John 5:2–3). God knows those traveling up that narrow road by name: "God the *Father knew you and chose you long ago and His Spirit made you holy. As a result, you obeyed Him and have been cleansed by the blood of Jesus"* (see 1 Peter 1:2).

The narrow road is, by no means, an easy road. It is probably as long as the broad, wide road. But the narrow road might have some stumbling blocks all along the way. The traveler might stumble and possibly skin a knee, or become hounded by evil spirits along the way. But he knows that God's presence is with him because he trusts his promise to be with him always even to the end of his journey. God's power and provisions have been with him in times past; there-fore, he knows his presence will be with him throughout eternity. All along the tedious journey, his spirit hears the Lord saying, *"Don't be afraid, for I am with you. Don't be discouraged, for I am your God. I will strengthen you and help you. I will hold you up with my victorious right hand"* (see Isaiah 41:10), and he becomes strengthened. I imagine the homeward-bound travelers feel the pressure of a hand lifting him up from the ground. His steps are probably lighter, and his heart is filled with joy as he focuses on Jesus, who will be standing at the gate, waiting to welcome him home!

As we near the culmination of *Under the Influence*, now would be a good time to ask yourself, "Which road have I been traveling on? Who has influenced my life the most?" Satan influences his followers to travel *down* that broad, wide road that is filled with all manner of worldly things to attract your attention. Or have you traveled *up* the narrow road with some difficulties disbursed with some joy along the way? The road you are traveling on will determine who is influencing you right now. It is not too late to change courses and follow Jesus. *He is* the way.

Are your eyes and ears open to the transforming truth that can set you free? Prophecies are being fulfilled at this very moment. Waves of epidemics, outbreaks of afflicting plagues, and uncontrollable viruses are marching across the physical world unhindered.

Don't be like the rebellious people to whom God sent Jeremiah to speak. He asked, *"To whom can I give warning? Who will I listen when I speak? Their ears are closed and they cannot hear"* (see Jeremiah 6:10). Or among those to whom Zephaniah was sent to speak of a coming judgment. Here was the Lord's message, *"Because you have sinned against the Lord. I will make you grope around like the blind"* (see Zephaniah 1:17).

Satan, who is the god of this world, has blinded the minds of those who don't believe. They are not able to see the glorious light of the Good News (see 2 Corinthians 4:4). However, God's grace (withholding judgment for what one deserves) and his mercy (giving people something that they don't deserve) abounds forevermore. There is still room at the cross for you!

# Author's Notation

Writing *Under the Influence* has been quite a phenomenal experience for me.

While preparing this manuscript to send to a publisher, I was amazed, grateful, and humbled by the Holy Spirit's guidance throughout this divinely appointed journey. I've been blessed to publish a few books in times past. But this is the first book that I have ever endeavor to write totally by faith. My personal knowledge was limited, but just whispering from the depths of my heart, "*I trust you, Lord,*" every time I sat down to write, amazed me at the outcome.

I remembered reading Jeremiah 33:3: "*Call to me and I will answer you and tell you great and unsearchable things you do not know*" (*KJV*). As I reviewed the last chapter of this manuscript, I realized that I had *experienced* God telling me unsearchable things involving the coronavirus long before it became a pandemic.

The last chapter of this manuscript was written in February 2020. While documenting Jesus's account of things that would occur during the last days, the term pestilence came up. That was when I learned that pestilence was a widespread infection! It was around March 11, 2020, when the virus was declared a pandemic! Even today, there are still many *unsearchable* things about the virus that scientists and doctors do not know!

I believe that this journey was previously charted for me, and I never knew what awaited me around the next corner. I traveled fearlessly, even though there were many stumbling blocks along some of the dark passageways on the journey. I had been studying from the same daily devotional guide for almost three years. The writer focused on God's power, his presence, and his protection throughout the guide. By the time this manuscript came to fruition, my relationship with the Lord was grounded and rooted.

With much joy and gratitude,
Margaret L. Blanchard

# About the Author

The author of *Under the Influence* has written three other Christian books, including *The Birth of a Christian*, which sold out of her first printing following a speaking engagement. She is a retired ob-gyn oncology nursing supervisor. She lives in Roswell, Georgia, with her husband where she teaches Sunday school. She has written a training manual for the church's outreach ministry where she has been a member for over two decades.

Writing began as a hobby for the author when she was very young, and it continues to bring her much joy, especially when she has an opportunity to share the Word of God with readers.

CPSIA information can be obtained
at www.ICGtesting.com
Printed in the USA
BVHW030006080621
608952BV00002B/215